is the foundation of freedom, justice and peace in the world, Whereas disregard... human

is the foundation of freedom, justice and peace in the world, Whereas dis... contempt for human

human beings shall enjoy freedom of speech and belief and freedom from fear and want has been

which human beings shall enjoy freedom of speech and belief and freedom from fear and want has been

recourse, as a last resort, to rebellion against tyranny and oppression, that human rights should be

recourse, as a last resort, to rebellion against tyranny and oppression, that human rights should be

Whereas the peoples of the United Nations have in the Charter reaffirmed their faith in fundamental

the peoples of the United Nations have in the Charter reaffirmed their faith in fundamental

ined to promote social progress and better standards of life in larger freedom, Whereas Member States

promote social progress and better standards of life in larger freedom, Whereas Member States

observance of human rights and fundamental freedoms, Whereas a common understanding of these rights

observance of human rights and fundamental freedoms, Whereas a common understanding of these rights

bly, Proclaims this Universal Declaration of Human Rights as a common standard of achievement for

Proclaims this Universal Declaration of Human Rights as a common standard of achievement for

ntly in mind, shall strive by teaching and education to promote respect for these rights and freedoms

in mind, shall strive by teaching and education to promote respect for these rights

e, both among the peoples of Member States themselves and among the peoples of territories under

both among the peoples of Member States themselves and among the peoples of territories under

W9-BTF-684

Eleanor Roosevelt:

Aunt M...
Uncle ...

Freedom's Champion

Letter to the Reader

Dear Reader,

The story of Eleanor Roosevelt is the story of modern America. Her life spanned the years 1884-1962—a period of time that saw some of the most far-reaching changes ever experienced by this nation. She actively participated in such history-making events as the Great Depression, two world wars, and the civil-rights movement. When friends urged Eleanor to slow down at age 75, she declared: "Life is meant to be lived." She continued taking part in world and national affairs for another two years.

To help you place Eleanor Roosevelt's life in the larger framework of history, we have provided you with two timelines at the start of each chapter. By studying the timelines before reading a chapter, you will see how history shaped Eleanor's life, and how she, in turn, shaped history.

As you read, you will notice many indented paragraphs and passages in quotation marks. These are quotations by Eleanor Roosevelt or people who knew her. These voices from the past help bring the story alive and encourage you to see history through Eleanor's eyes.

In the margins of the book you will find on-page definitions for highlighted words that may be unfamiliar to you. This feature allows you to stay involved in the story as you add new words to your vocabulary. You will also find photographs that help tell the story. Glance at these photos as you read, and witness the changes in Eleanor Roosevelt and in the world in which she lived.

Eleanor Roosevelt reached out to young people throughout her life. Her fondest wish was that the story of her life would continue to touch young people for years to come. We hope that you enjoy reading *Eleanor Roosevelt: Freedom's Champion*.

The Authors

Eleanor Roosevelt:

Freedom's
Champion

Deborah A. Parks and Melva L. Ware

Time Life Education   Alexandria, Virginia

Key Events in Eleanor Roosevelt's Life

	Key Events Around the World

Key Events in Eleanor Roosevelt's Life

Key Events Around the World

Eleanor Roosevelt's Life	Years	Around the World
1884 — Anna Eleanor Roosevelt is born into a prominent, wealthy family in the state of New York.	**1884-1893**	1886 — Chiricahua Apache chief Geronimo is captured by U.S. troops; the Indian Wars end.
1899 — Eleanor is sent to Allenswood School for Girls in England.	**1893-1902**	1896 — The U.S. Supreme Court rules in *Plessy v. Ferguson* that states have the right to provide "separate but equal" facilities for education, public accommodations, and transit.
1903 — Eleanor becomes engaged to Franklin Delano Roosevelt, her fifth cousin. They marry two years later on St. Patrick's Day.	**1902-1905**	1905 — Albert Einstein proposes his theory of relativity: $E=mc^2$.
1910 — Eleanor moves the family to Albany, New York, when Franklin is elected to the New York state senate.	**1905-1918**	1914 — World War I begins in Europe. The United States enters the war three years later, after German submarine attacks on U.S. ships.
1921 — Franklin is stricken with polio while vacationing at Campobello Island.	**1918-1921**	1918 — On November 11, Germany signs a treaty with the Allies, ending World War I.
1922 — Eleanor joins the Women's Trade Union League, founded in 1903.	**1921-1924**	1924 — Native Americans are granted full U.S. citizenship rights, including the right to vote.
1932 — Franklin is elected president. Eleanor wants to be "plain, ordinary Mrs. Roosevelt" as first lady.	**1924-1932**	1932 — Amelia Earhart is the first woman to fly solo across the Atlantic Ocean.
1933 — As first lady, Eleanor is the first to hold press conferences—and for women reporters only. She also begins writing her syndicated column, "My Day."	**1932-1936**	1935 — President Roosevelt establishes the Rural Electrification Administration (REA) to bring electricity to all Americans.
1936 — Franklin is reelected president. Eleanor continues as an active first lady.	**1936-1941**	1939 — Germany invades Poland, beginning World War II. Two years later, Japan bombs Pearl Harbor and the United States enters the war.
1943 — Eleanor travels to the South Pacific to boost troop morale. Two years later, Franklin dies of a stroke at his polio treatment center in Warm Springs, Georgia.	**1941-1945**	1945 — Adolf Hitler commits suicide, and Germany surrenders. Japan surrenders when the United States drops atomic bombs on two of its cities. World War II is over.
1948 — As United Nations Representative for the United States, Eleanor wins passage of the Universal Declaration of Human Rights.	**1945-1962**	1962 — The year Eleanor dies, Cesar Chavez forms the National Farm Workers Association to promote the rights of migrant farmworkers.

Eleanor Roosevelt: Freedom's Champion

Bright Moments
Sad Times

Chapter I

1884 - 1893

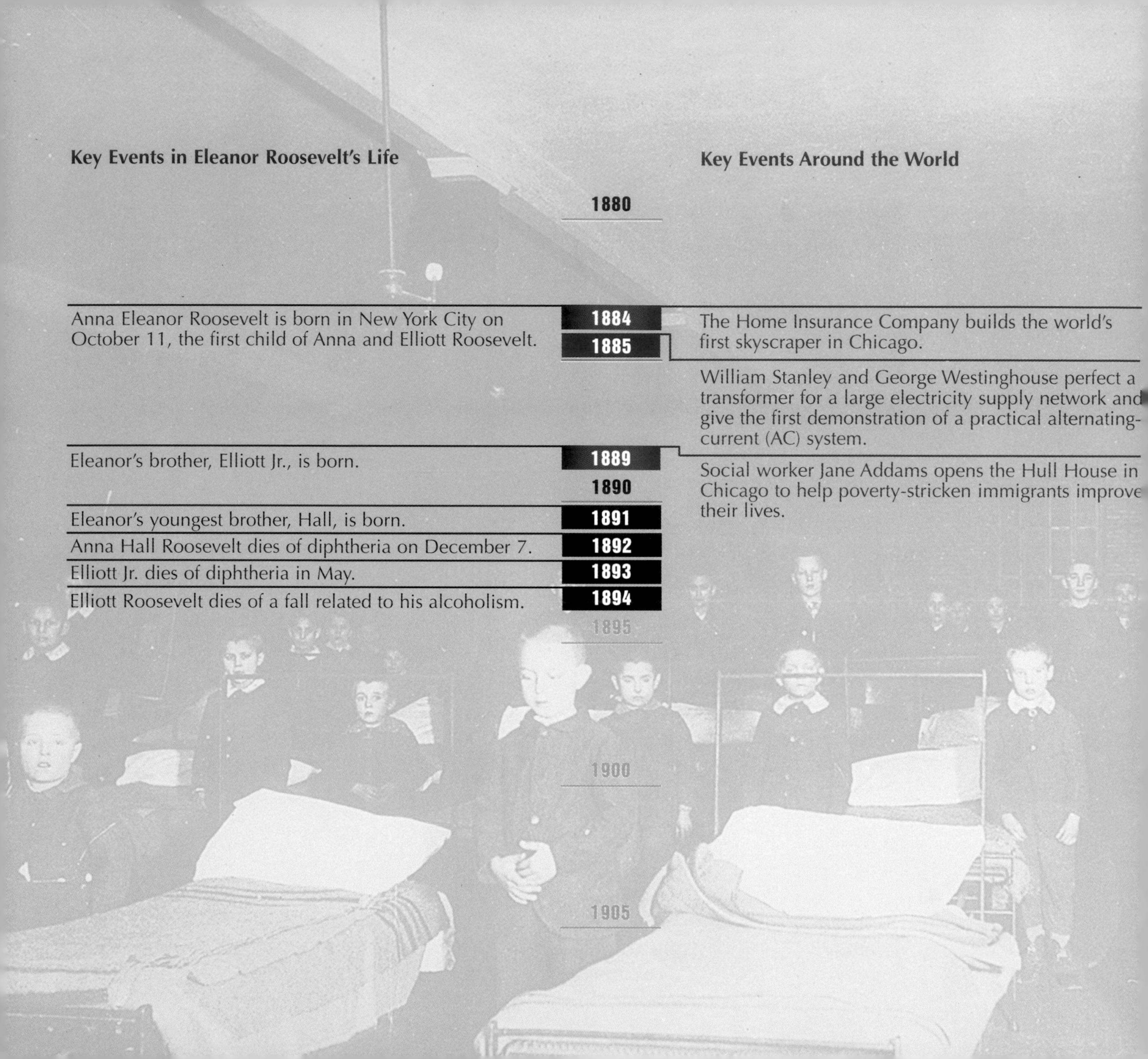

Key Events in Eleanor Roosevelt's Life

Key Events Around the World

1880

| | 1884 | Anna Eleanor Roosevelt is born in New York City on October 11, the first child of Anna and Elliott Roosevelt. |

Anna Eleanor Roosevelt is born in New York City on October 11, the first child of Anna and Elliott Roosevelt.

1884
1885

The Home Insurance Company builds the world's first skyscraper in Chicago.

William Stanley and George Westinghouse perfect a transformer for a large electricity supply network and give the first demonstration of a practical alternating-current (AC) system.

Eleanor's brother, Elliott Jr., is born.

1889

1890

Social worker Jane Addams opens the Hull House in Chicago to help poverty-stricken immigrants improve their lives.

Eleanor's youngest brother, Hall, is born.

1891

Anna Hall Roosevelt dies of diphtheria on December 7.

1892

Elliott Jr. dies of diphtheria in May.

1893

Elliott Roosevelt dies of a fall related to his alcoholism.

1894

1895

1900

1905

The minute young Eleanor Roosevelt heard her father come through the front door, she ran from her bedroom and down two flights of stairs, to tumble into his waiting arms.

Elliott Roosevelt called Eleanor "Little Nell," after a character in a Charles Dickens book. Eleanor was proud of this special name. "I . . . knew it was a term of affection," she recalled, "and I never doubted that I stood first in his heart."

When Eleanor was born—on October 11, 1884—Elliott described her as a "miracle from Heaven." At home, he showered his daughter with affection. Unfortunately, Elliott spent much of his time away, visiting friends or traveling to faraway places.

Because he was away for long periods, Elliott tried to make his times with Eleanor memorable, and she remembered them vividly. In 1890, he took Eleanor and her mother, Anna Hall Roosevelt, to Venice, Italy. There he played gondolier, singing Italian songs in a booming voice as he guided his wife and daughter through the city's canals.

As Eleanor grew up, she would cling to such bright moments as "the high points of my existence." She clung to them amid family tragedies that brought her overwhelming sadness. Perhaps the greatest source of her sorrow was none other than her beloved father. In years to come, Eleanor would learn a terrible truth: Her father suffered from alcoholism. No matter how hard he tried to break its grip, he never completely escaped. Elliott's struggle left its mark on his family—and on the daughter who adored him.

Photo courtesy of Franklin Roosevelt Library, NPx 65-25.

Eleanor with her father, Elliott, and one of his dogs at Hempstead, New York, in 1889.

Gondolier:

A boatman who steers a long, flat-bottomed boat on the canals of Venice, Italy.

Alcoholism:

An addiction to alcoholic beverages that steadily damages the heart, liver, and nervous system.

Society's Child

Eleanor came from a world of privilege and wealth. The 1883 marriage of her parents, 23-year-old Elliott Roosevelt and 19-year-old Anna Hall, brought together two of New York's oldest and richest families. Writing about the world in which they lived, Eleanor said:

> In that Society . . . [y]ou accepted invitations to dine and to dance with the right people only, you lived where you would be in their midst. You thought seriously about your children's education, you read the books that everybody read. . . . In short, you conformed. . . .

Elliott did not always conform, however, and that was part of his charm. He loved exotic travel and adventure. Anna, famed for her beauty and grace, saw Elliott as a dashing young man who offered a life that was a welcome contrast to her strict upbringing.

Although there were rumors of Elliott's heavy drinking, Anna ignored them. Instead, she wrote Elliott a letter on the eve of their marriage: "Believe me, I am quite strong enough to face, with you, the storms of this life."

The storms of this life proved far stronger than Anna had imagined. Within two months of their marriage, Elliott's mother died, sending him into a deep depression. He drank heavily and often stayed out all night with friends. Anna begged him to seek help for his drinking.

When Eleanor was born, Elliott and Anna could afford to hire cooks and nursemaids to care for her and her two younger brothers, Elliott Jr. and Hall. But the family money could not protect the children

Elliott and Anna Roosevelt sitting for a formal portrait early in their marriage.

Photo courtesy of Franklin Roosevelt Library, NPx 91-174 (69).

from the unhappiness that filled their home. Describing her early years, Eleanor wrote:

> *I was a shy, solemn child even at the age of two, and I am*
> *sure that even when I danced, which I did frequently,*
> *I never smiled.*

"Granny" and Her Mother

Eleanor's mother tried to escape her painful marriage through a never ending round of social activities. Anna grew more distant from Eleanor. If she saw Eleanor, with her sorrowful eyes, standing in the doorway to her room, she would snap at her: "Come in, Granny."

Eleanor's mother called her that name even in front of visitors. Over tea, Anna once confided to a friend: "She is such a funny child, so old-fashioned, that we always call her 'Granny.' " Eleanor vividly recalled how she felt when she heard those words: "I wanted to sink through the floor in shame."

Eleanor wilted under her mother's criticism. She compared her plain appearance with her mother's glamour. In awe of her mother, Eleanor remarked:

> *I . . . remember well the thrill of watching her dress to go out in*
> *the evenings. She looked so beautiful, I was grateful to be*
> *allowed to touch her dress or her jewels or anything else that*
> *was part of the vision which I admired. . . .*

Photo courtesy of Franklin Roosevelt Library, NPx 47-96-3532.

Photo courtesy of Franklin Roosevelt Library, NPx 65-148.

Eleanor's father, Elliott Roosevelt.

Top: Anna Hall Roosevelt wearing the tiger-claw necklace given to her by her husband, Elliott.

Tutors:

Teachers hired as in-home instructors
to give personal, one-on-one instruction.

Photo courtesy of Franklin Roosevelt Library, NPx 81-93.

Eleanor's mother, Anna, in 1890.

When Anna hired tutors for her daughter, Eleanor imagined that it was to "compensate for my looks." She studied hard but could not seem to please her mother. Eleanor guessed at all sorts of reasons for her mother's coldness—perhaps she spoke French poorly, or she spelled words incorrectly.

Anna's real concern was not her daughter's imagined faults but Elliott's inability to stop drinking. In 1891, newspaper headlines announced that alcoholism had put Elliott in a French hospital. Anna tried to keep the scandal a secret from her children. Lying in bed, Eleanor strained to hear her mother's hushed conversations:

> *I acquired many a strange and garbled idea of the troubles*
> *which were going on around me. Something was wrong with*
> *my father, and from my point of view nothing could be wrong*
> *with him.*

Eleanor tried to ease her fears by focusing on her mother's needs. Anna complained of blinding headaches and would lie in her bedroom with the curtains tightly shut. Eleanor sat on her mother's bed and gently stroked Anna's head. She later wrote:

> *Perhaps even as a child there was something soothing in my*
> *touch, for she was willing to let me sit there for hours on end.*
> *As with all children, the feeling that I was useful was perhaps*
> *the greatest joy I experienced.*

A Brother's Keeper

Elliott's older brother, Theodore, believed that Anna sheltered Elliott too much. He used her illness as an excuse to intervene. In January 1892, Theodore (known as TR) sailed to France to bring Elliott back to America for more treatment. He told Elliott that Anna did not wish to see him until he was well, and he arranged for Elliott to live away from his family for a period of two years.

As Elliott regained his health, he wrote letters of apology to Anna. Anna feared Elliott's return. Her declining health made her feel tired. Elliott sensed her fears and tried to calm them, but he ran out of time.

In late November 1892, Anna entered the hospital for surgery. Before the surgery, she muttered that her life was so sad that she wanted to die. Her wish came true when she developed diphtheria and slipped into unconsciousness. On December 7, at age 29, Anna passed away. A telegram summoned Elliott to the funeral.

Multiple Losses

Eight-year-old Eleanor barely reacted when her cousin, Susie Parish, brought the news of her mother's death. When Elliott came for the funeral, he talked to his daughter of his sadness and of their need to remain close. Eleanor's spirits soared. "There started that day a feeling which never left me—that he and I . . . some day would have a life of our own together."

Elliott Jr., Hall, and Eleanor with their father, Elliott, in 1892.

Diphtheria:
A contagious disease that inflames the lungs, heart, and nervous system, making it difficult to breathe.

Elliott Roosevelt with his terriers.

Will:
A legal document that identifies how ownership of a person's property and belongings should be distributed after death.

Photo courtesy of Franklin Roosevelt Library, NPx 47-96:2523.

Photo courtesy of Franklin Roosevelt Library, NPx 72-235.

Eleanor Roosevelt, ambassador to the United Nations, global peacemaker, human-rights activist, and grandmother.

Top: Eleanor and her brother Elliott Jr. in 1891.

Eleanor did not yet know that Anna's will named her mother, Mary Hall, as the guardian for her children. Anna did not believe that Elliott could be a proper father. Elliott would have to ask Mary Hall for permission to visit his children.

Eleanor lived for her father's visits. She could not see that Elliott was fighting his final battle with alcoholism. He almost gave up in 1893, when three-year-old Elliott Jr. died of diphtheria. Elliott visited Eleanor less and less, sending letters instead. On August 13, 1894, Elliott wrote Eleanor his last letter:

> *I have . . . been . . . quite ill, at intervals not able to move from my bed for days. . . . Give my love to Grandma and [Hall]. . . . I hope my little girl is well. . . . and never forget I love you.*

The next day, Elliott died from a drunken fall. At first, Eleanor refused to believe the news. Then she broke down in a flood of tears and cried herself to sleep. When she woke up, Eleanor found herself daydreaming of her father: "I knew in my mind that father was dead, and yet I lived with him more closely . . . than I had when he was alive."

Eleanor Roosevelt was not yet 10 years old. Over the next 68 years, this shy, dreamy orphan would grow into one of the most influential women in the world—first lady of the United States, global peacemaker, and champion of human rights. If her life had any lesson at all, Eleanor would later say, it was "to show that one can . . . overcome obstacles that seem [huge] if one is willing to face the fact that they must be overcome."

Sprouting
Wings

Chapter 2

1893 - 1902

Key Events in Eleanor Roosevelt's Life

Key Events Around the World

1890

Eleanor and Hall move to Grandmother Hall's home in New York City. **1893**

1895 Guglielmo Marconi develops the wireless telegraph.

1897 The United States signs an annexation treaty that will make the Hawaiian Islands a territory in 1900.

Eleanor first dances with her fifth cousin, Franklin, at the annual Roosevelt Christmas party. **1898**

1899 Theodore Roosevelt gains national attention by leading the "Rough Riders" into battle in Cuba during the Spanish-American War.

Eleanor boards a ship headed to England, where she will enroll in Allenswood and meet Mlle. Souvestre. **1900**

1901 *The Wonderful Wizard of Oz* is written by a Chicago newspaperman, Lyman Frank Baum.

Grandmother Hall calls Eleanor back to New York to make her debut in society, just before her 18th birthday. **1902**

Theodore Roosevelt becomes president when President McKinley is assassinated.

1905 The teddy bear, named after President Theodore (Teddy) Roosevelt, becomes an overnight sensation.

1910

1915

The death of Eleanor's parents placed her in the hands of her grandmother, Mary Ludlow Livingston Hall.

When Eleanor and her little brother, Hall, joined their grandmother in 1893, they found her unable to handle the four rebellious young adults who still lived with her. The two boys, Vallie and Eddie, drank heavily and got into fights. The two remaining daughters, Maude and Edith, smoked cigarettes (not accepted for young ladies of this time), and they had a number of men competing for their attention.

Eleanor saw her aunts and uncles as free spirits. During summers at Oak Terrace—the Hall country home in Tivoli, New York—Eleanor's "uncontrollable" aunts and uncles taught her how to jump a pony, ride a bike, row a boat, and drive a two-wheeled pony cart. And they inspired her sense of adventure. Once, Eleanor and Hall climbed out a third-story window and walked on a rain gutter all around the house, not realizing the rain gutter was made of tin and could easily have fallen off the house.

Eleanor's grandmother, Mary Hall.

A Proper Upbringing

Grandmother Hall was determined to give her two grandchildren the discipline her own children lacked. As Eleanor put it, "We were brought up on the principle that 'no' was easier to say than 'yes.'" On Sundays, Mary Hall escorted the children to church; at home, later in the day, she taught them Bible verses and gathered the family for hymn singing.

Eleanor and her bicycle, with her Aunt Maude at Oak Terrace in 1894.

Photo courtesy of Franklin Roosevelt Library, NPx 58-273.

Eleanor in her usual attire at Oak Terrace in 1894.

Photo courtesy of Franklin Roosevelt Library, NPx 48-22-4289(3).

A teenage Eleanor with her brother, Hall, in 1898.

She hired tutors to teach Eleanor music, writing, French, and German. Eleanor was especially fond of writing. When she was 14 years old, she wrote an essay titled "Ambition" that gave a glimpse of her potential as a leader:

> *Of course it is easier to have no ambition and . . . never try to do grand and great things. . . . [But is it] better . . . to leave the world a blank as if one had never come? It seems to me that we should leave some mark upon the world and not just pass away[,] for what good can that do?*

By her teens, Eleanor stood almost six feet tall. Self-conscious about her height, she sometimes slumped over when she stood. Her grandmother sent her to ballet classes, made her practice walking straight, and even forced her to wear a back brace for a year.

Eleanor suffered other humiliations from the childish, old-fashioned clothes she had to wear. Her grandmother dressed her in plain, short dresses with big bows in the back. She wore long, black stockings and high-button shoes. Most young women Eleanor's age were wearing stylish long dresses. Eleanor's clothes made her feel even more self-conscious.

The Rowdy Roosevelts

Mary Hall's efforts to protect her grandchildren extended to the rowdy family of Theodore Roosevelt. Mary saw TR's family—especially his oldest daughter Alice—as far too outspoken and willful.

For much of Eleanor's teenage years, the Hall and Roosevelt families met only on rare occasions, perhaps one time in the summer and another time at Christmas. But whenever Eleanor visited Sagamore Hill, the Roosevelt home at Oyster Bay on Long Island, TR (or Uncle Ted, as she called him) would welcome her with shouts of joy and give her crushing bear hugs.

Alice resented the attention her father showered on Eleanor. She disliked Eleanor's shyness and thought Eleanor was boring. Eleanor, however, felt intimidated by Alice's "sophisticated and grown-up" ways.

The differences between the two girls were most visible at the family's annual Christmas party. As Alice flirted with the boys and spun around the dance floor in an elegant evening gown, Eleanor leaned against a wall in her childish short dress. But the year she was 14, one of her cousins asked her to dance. He was a 16-year-old student at Groton, an exclusive boys' school in Connecticut. "I still remember my gratitude . . . ," said Eleanor years later, "when he came and asked me to dance. . . ." Her first dance partner was her fifth cousin, Franklin Delano Roosevelt.

Sailing to a New Life

Mary Hall realized that she could not shelter Eleanor forever. A year after the dance with Franklin, she told Eleanor: "Your mother wanted you to go to boarding school in Europe. And I have decided to send you. . . ." She picked Allenswood, a girls' school near London, England.

Eleanor at age 14, just before leaving for Allenswood.

Top: Franklin Delano Roosevelt at the Delano family estate in Fairhaven, Massachusetts, in 1897.

Photo courtesy of Franklin Roosevelt Library, NPx 64-376.

Photo courtesy of Franklin Roosevelt Library, NPx 81-18.

Mademoiselle:

A proper title for an unmarried Frenchwoman.

Mlle. Souvestre in her study with some of her students.

Top: A portrait of Mlle. Souvestre around 1900.

In September 1899, 14-year-old Eleanor boarded a steamship bound for England. Her Aunt Tissie—Elizabeth Livingston Hall Mortimer—traveled with her. Tissie had lived in London for many years, and she promised to escort Eleanor to the school that would be her home for the next three years. When they arrived at the school, Aunt Tissie met briefly with the school's headmistress, Mademoiselle (Mlle.) Souvestre, and headed back to London.

The Allenswood Adventure

"I felt lost and very lonely when she drove away," Eleanor admitted. The feeling soon passed, however. For the first time in her life, Eleanor found herself living with other girls her own age. Eleanor's roommate, Marjorie Bennett, showed her around the school and explained the rules.

Mlle. Souvestre seemed to have even more rules than Eleanor's grandmother. Students had to keep their rooms in order, and they had to speak only in French all day long! There were schedules for everything, from meals, to classes, to baths.

Despite the rules, Eleanor adapted quickly to Allenswood. Thanks to years of tutoring in French, she arrived at school fluent in the language. Her seriousness, a drawback at home, was a plus at Allenswood. Classmates thought she was more grown up than they were and looked to her as a leader.

Mlle. Souvestre also liked Eleanor immediately and saw her great potential. Living at a time when women lacked many rights—including the right to vote, Mlle. Souvestre believed women must be educated.

For change to take place, women had to learn leadership skills. She encouraged her students to think independently and speak their minds freely. A former student described her teaching methods as:

> Brilliant speech [that] darted here and there with the agility and grace of a hummingbird. . . . she communicated a . . . fire which warmed and colored [her students'] whole lives. To sit at her [table] was an education in itself.

Eleanor soon won an honored seat at Mlle. Souvestre's table. At nightly meals, she found herself engaged in sparkling conversations. The brilliant teacher helped Eleanor overcome her shyness and challenged her to express her ideas and feelings. According to Eleanor, "She had an eagle eye which penetrated right through to your backbone and . . . took in everything about you."

Eleanor came alive at Allenswood. Taking on a difficult program of study, she excelled at independent research and writing. Her confidence grew and she soon became one of Mlle. Souvestre's star pupils. Eleanor later wrote: "This was the first time in . . . my life that all my fears left me."

Although other students at Allenswood saw Eleanor as a leader, she never forgot what it was like to be a lonely outsider. In a letter to Eleanor's grandmother, Mlle. Souvestre reported: "She is full of sympathy for all those who live with her." Such compassion would become Eleanor's lifelong trait.

Allenswood as it looked when Eleanor arrived in 1899.

An Allenswood class picture. Eleanor is in the back row, third from the right.

Photo courtesy of Franklin Roosevelt Library, NPx 65-26(B).

Eleanor on a holiday break from Allenswood, in St. Moritz, Switzerland.

Debut:

A formal introduction to society.

Exploring the World

From 1899 to 1902, Eleanor's education extended far beyond the classrooms of Allenswood. Unlike other students, Eleanor did not go home during school breaks. Instead, she traveled in Europe with her Aunt Tissie or Mlle. Souvestre.

> *Mlle. Souvestre taught me . . . on these journeys . . . that the way to make young people responsible is to throw real responsibility on them. . . . The packing and unpacking for both of us was up to me. . . . I looked up trains, got the tickets, [and] made all the detailed arrangements necessary for comfortable traveling.*

Eleanor described the trips with Mlle. Souvestre as "one of the most momentous things that happened in my education." The headmistress took Eleanor to small hotels off the beaten path, ordered local foods, and changed plans at the spur of the moment. Such experiences made a deep and lasting impression on Eleanor: "Never again would I be the rigid little person I had been."

In 1902, Mary Hall wrote to Mlle. Souvestre that Eleanor needed to come home and make her debut in New York society. Mlle. Souvestre worried that Eleanor might forget all that she had learned. In a letter to Eleanor shortly before her debut, Mlle. Souvestre wrote:

> *Protect yourself . . . against . . . [the] worldly pleasures which are going to beckon you. And even when success comes, . . . bear in mind that there are more . . . enviable joys than to be among the most sought-after women at a ball. . . .*

Different Worlds

Chapter 3

1902 - 1905

Key Events in Eleanor Roosevelt's Life

Key Events Around the World

1900

1902

Eleanor makes her debut on December 11, 1902.

1903

Eleanor is engaged to Franklin Delano Roosevelt, her fifth cousin "once removed."

1904

The Wright Brothers fly the first gasoline-powered airplane at Kitty Hawk, N.C.

1905

Eleanor does volunteer work for the Junior League and the Consumers' League in New York City.

Mary McLeod Bethune opens Daytona Normal and Industrial Institute for Negro Girls (later renamed Bethune-Cookman College) in Daytona Beach, Florida.

President Theodore Roosevelt is awarded the Nobel Peace Prize for his work as a mediator between Russia and Japan.

1910

1915

1920

1925

$\mathcal{E}$leanor returned to New York in June 1902. She dreaded the December 11 Assembly Ball when New York debutantes presented themselves to society. After the ball, there would be "coming out" parties hosted by the families of other debutantes. As a member of a prominent family, Eleanor could not escape her social duties. "Not to 'come out' was unthinkable," she later reflected.

Debutante:

A young woman who is formally introduced to society.

Family Nightmares

Eleanor spent a miserable summer at Oak Terrace with the Halls. "My Uncle Vallie, who had been so kind to me when I was a child, had been slipping rapidly into the habits of an habitual drinker." On some drinking sprees, Vallie would grab a rifle and shoot at anything that moved. Eleanor and her brother, Hall, learned to crouch behind tree trunks whenever they walked across the yard. Eleanor's Uncle Eddie, who was now married, sometimes returned home to join Vallie in these drinking binges. "That . . . summer was not a very good preparation for being a . . . debutante," she wrote.

In September, Eleanor and her grandmother took Hall to Groton, the boarding school where their cousin Franklin had gone. Were it not for Eleanor, Hall would have been abandoned at Groton. Her grandmother was too distracted by Vallie's drinking problem. Eleanor recalled:

A portrait of Eleanor to announce her debut at age 18.

Top: A high-society lawn party at Newport, Rhode Island, in 1902.

Colonel Theodore Roosevelt, 1st Cavalry, U.S. Army, in 1898.

Top: President William McKinley.

Assassin:
A person who commits murder for political reasons.

Real responsibility for . . . [my] young brother was slipping very rapidly from her hands into mine. She never went again to see him at school and I began to go up every term for a week end, which was what all good parents were expected to do. I kept this up through the six years he was there. . . .

Later that month, Eleanor was sent to live with her young aunt, Edith Hall, in Grandmother Hall's townhouse in New York City. Separated from Hall and from her friends at Allenswood, Eleanor told her Aunt Corinne she felt she had "no real home."

Roosevelts in the News

Wrapped up in family problems, Eleanor's grandmother could do nothing about her granddaughter's "coming out." She didn't have to worry. As soon as Eleanor turned 18 on October 11, she found her name splashed across the society pages of New York newspapers. Not only was she a member of the Hall and Roosevelt families, she was now the niece of the president!

In 1900, President William McKinley had chosen Eleanor's Uncle Ted as his vice presidential running mate. Five months after McKinley was sworn in as president, an assassin's bullet ended his life and thrust Theodore Roosevelt (TR) into the presidency. At age 43, TR was the youngest person ever to hold the office.

With the Roosevelt name so prominent in the news, Eleanor felt overwhelmed by her upcoming debut. Her cousin, Alice—nicknamed Princess Alice by the press—had celebrated her debut with a huge party at the White House the previous year. Eleanor knew she could not measure up to the celebrated debutantes in her family: "By no stretch of the imagination could I fool myself into thinking that I was a popular debutante!"

Alice Roosevelt as a young debutante.

Utter Agony

The night of the Assembly Ball, Eleanor put on the fashionable dress her Aunt Tissie had bought for her in Paris. Its soft blue color brought out her striking blue eyes. "I imagine that I was well dressed," Eleanor later recalled, "but there was absolutely nothing about me to attract anybody's attention."

She described the ball as "utter agony" and left the dance early, certain that she was a social failure. Not everybody saw Eleanor in the same light. Several of the young men who met Eleanor at the dance took a serious interest in her. Even her jealous cousin Alice had a more favorable view of Eleanor's social debut:

> She was always making herself out to be an ugly duckling but
> she was really rather attractive. Tall, rather coltish-looking,
> with masses of pale, gold hair rippling to below her waist, and
> really lovely blue eyes.

Eleanor with her cousins
Helen Roosevelt and Muriel Robbins
in 1903.

Photo courtesy of Library of Congress, LC-US262-46408.

New York City settlement house, 1890.

Junior League:

A women's organization founded in the early 20th century to carry out volunteer projects that helped those in need.

Settlement house:

An apartment building where immigrants could find temporary shelter, receive food, or get help finding a job.

But Eleanor had too many things on her mind to become the typical debutante: "That first winter . . . nearly brought me to a state of nervous collapse." Responsibility for her brother and the chaos in the Hall household had made Eleanor an even more serious young woman. She wanted to make some friends like those she had at Allenswood—young women who thought of other things than debutante balls and party dresses.

Meaningful Work

In 1902, Eleanor's desire to meet other serious-minded young women led her to join New York City's Junior League. Members could participate by working at a settlement house on Rivington Street in New York City's Lower East Side or by raising money to help fund the settlement house program. Only a handful of women wanted to work in the poor neighborhoods, where most immigrants lived. Eleanor was one of these brave volunteers.

Eleanor remembered that her father taught her the importance of "[being] kind to the poor . . . and [doing] something for the needy." From the age of six, she had helped Elliott serve Thanksgiving dinners to the poor and had gone with him to the Children's Aid Society. There, Eleanor had seen children dressed in rags, with no food and no place to live. These early impressions came back to her as she visited the Rivington Street settlement house.

Conquering Fear

Several family members tried to talk Eleanor out of working in the slums, but she ignored them. Eleanor alarmed her family even more by refusing to travel to Rivington Street by private carriage. Instead, she traveled downtown by streetcar or elevated train. When she got off the train, she had to walk across the Bowery—a run-down part of the Lower East Side. Describing her trip, Eleanor wrote: "I often waited on a corner . . . , watching, with a great deal of [fear], . . . but the children interested me enormously."

The children at the settlement house drew Eleanor back day after day. She taught classes in exercise and dance. She stayed from the time school let out until the early evening. "I feel sure I was a very poor teacher," said Eleanor, "for I had no experience." If this was true, the children did not notice. In fact, one little girl invited her home to meet her father. "I still remember the glow of pride that ran through me," Eleanor declared.

In 1903, Eleanor also joined the Consumers' League, headed by Maud Nathan. The Consumers' League tried to improve the working conditions of wage-earning women and children. Eleanor saw women who worked in clothing factories and department stores up to 14 hours a day, six days a week, for weekly wages of only six dollars. She visited her first sweatshop. Here, she saw children as young as four and five years old making artificial flowers and feathers for pennies a day. They worked, said Eleanor, "until they fell off their benches, just asleep." She never forgot the sight.

Pitt and Rivington Streets, Lower East Side, New York City, 1915.

Top: A young girl working in a factory in the early 20th century.

Consumers' League:
Founded in 1899, it consisted of a group of women who lobbied to improve the working conditions of wage-earning women and children.

Sweatshop:
A factory that pays its employees low wages to work long hours in a poorly ventilated working environment.

Photo courtesy of Franklin Roosevelt Library, NPx 48-22-3619(101).

Photo courtesy of Franklin Roosevelt Library, NPx 47-96-3562.

Springwood, the Roosevelt family house at Hyde Park, before it was remodeled in 1915.

Top: Franklin and Eleanor courting, on the porch of the Roosevelt family house at Campobello in 1904.

Eleanor cherished her volunteer work because it gave her a chance to help others—a goal that would motivate her throughout her life. The hours spent at the settlement house were the "nicest part of the day." Her hard work won the admiration of Franklin Roosevelt—the cousin who had danced with Eleanor when she was 14 years old. After meeting the grown-up Eleanor, he wrote in his journal: "E is an Angel."

Cousin Franklin

Eleanor and Franklin had renewed their friendship on a 1902 train ride up the Hudson River Valley. Eleanor was headed to Oak Terrace, her grandmother's home near Tivoli, New York. Franklin was headed to Springwood, the Roosevelt family estate in the town of Hyde Park. As Eleanor read a book, she heard someone call out her name. She watched the jaunty, good-looking young man walk toward her with his characteristic wide grin. They talked for nearly two hours. As the train neared Hyde Park, Franklin suggested that Eleanor go to the parlor car to meet his mother, Sara Delano Roosevelt.

Sara's appearance surprised Eleanor. Sara's husband had died two years earlier, but she was still dressed all in black. She peered at Eleanor through long, dark mourning veils that hung from her hat to the floor. She greeted Eleanor politely, chatted for a few minutes, and then asked Franklin to help her off the train at the Hyde Park station.

After their chance meeting, Eleanor and Franklin ran into each other more frequently. Franklin, a student at Harvard University in Cambridge, Massachusetts, showed up at many of the debutante balls that Eleanor so disliked. As Roosevelts, they both found their names on the guest lists for White House parties. After sitting near Eleanor at a 1903 New Year's party at the White House, Franklin wrote in his diary: "Sat near Eleanor. Very interesting day."

Throughout 1903, Eleanor and Franklin deepened their friendship through letters and visits. Eleanor especially liked the fact that Franklin took an interest in her settlement house work. He sometimes met her there after her classes and laughed at the openness of her students, particularly a little boy who called him her "feller." Once, he went with Eleanor to visit a young girl who had become sick. Franklin was shocked at the tenement conditions. He "could not believe human beings lived that way." Eleanor always believed these visits to the Rivington Street settlement house had a deep and lasting effect on Franklin.

The Rules of Courtship

In 1903, the rules of courtship were well understood by young single women. Eleanor explained:

> *You never allowed a man to give you a present except flowers or candy or possibly a book. . . . the idea that you would permit any man to kiss you before you were engaged . . . never even crossed my mind.*

Franklin Delano Roosevelt at age 22, Cambridge, Massachusetts, 1904.

Tenement:

A crowded apartment building or set of rooms, usually in poor condition, rented by low-income families.

New York City tenements, 233 East 107th Street, 1912.

Courting:

Dating someone seriously, with the intent of becoming engaged to marry. The period of time when two people are courting is called the courtship.

Franklin as a young boy with his adoring mother, Sara.

Top: Franklin on the stern of a sailboat at Campobello, 1904.

Franklin followed these rules carefully, but he made it increasingly clear that he was, in fact, courting Eleanor. His attention pleased yet surprised her. Why, she wondered, would this handsome 21-year-old Harvard student be so interested in her? Franklin answered this question, in part, by a remark he made to his mother. "Cousin Eleanor has a very good mind," he told Sara.

Mama's Boy

Franklin was an only child—the center of his parents' world. Sara and her husband, James Roosevelt, took Franklin wherever they went. When Franklin was eight years old, James suffered a heart attack and remained an invalid for the last 10 years of his life. Sara, more than 20 years younger than James, drew even closer to Franklin. She could not bear to send him to boarding school at Groton when he turned 12, so she kept him home an extra two years. When 14-year-old Franklin arrived at Groton, he was older than his classmates and never fit in—a secret he kept from Sara and James. After the death of her husband, Sara took an apartment in Boston to be near Franklin at Harvard. Franklin's closeness to his mother led some young women to view him as a "mama's boy."

Because Eleanor never teased Franklin, he shared his most secret feelings with her. He told Eleanor that "he often felt left out." Eleanor knew very well what it meant to be an outsider. She praised Franklin's successes: his membership in Hasty Pudding, Harvard's acting club; his feats in Harvard's rowing club; and his appointment as editor of the *Harvard Crimson*, the school's well-known newspaper.

In the fall of 1903, Franklin invited Eleanor to a Harvard football game. She was 19 years old and he was 21. Eleanor's aunt and cousin traveled with her as chaperones. During the weekend, the couple managed to slip away for a walk alone. By the time they returned, Franklin had proposed to Eleanor—and she had accepted.

Chaperones:

Older relatives or friends who accompany a young, unmarried woman to any social event attended by members of the opposite sex.

A Secret Engagement

The news stunned and disappointed Sara. She pleaded for Franklin and Eleanor to put off the engagement. Franklin had not yet finished his studies. She thought the couple was too young. What did they know about love? "I know my mind," Franklin responded.

Sara persuaded the couple to delay the announcement of their engagement for at least one year. In the meantime, she took Franklin and his roommate on a Caribbean cruise. She also tried to get him a job in London. Eleanor later confided: "At the time, of course, I resented [it]. . . . [But] Franklin's feelings did not change."

Franklin gave Eleanor an engagement ring on her 20th birthday, October 11, 1904. "You could not have found a ring I would have liked better," Eleanor declared. On December 1, New York newspapers announced the engagement and celebrated Eleanor as "attractive" and "unusually tall and fair," with "a charming grace of manner that has made her a favorite since her debut." Teddy Roosevelt promptly fired off a letter of congratulations to Franklin. "I am as fond of Eleanor as if she were my daughter. . . . May all good fortune attend you both, ever."

Eleanor wading in the water at Campobello with her Aunt Maude, 1904.

Photo courtesy of Franklin Roosevelt Library, NPx 47-96.2391.

Photo courtesy of Library of Congress, LC-USZ62-87234.

Theodore Roosevelt.

When Eleanor asked her Uncle Ted to give her away at the wedding, he said that he would be "DEE-lighted!" His acceptance promised to make the wedding the biggest event of the 1905 social season. Nobody could possibly guess that he would be blessing one of the most amazing political partnerships in U.S. history—a partnership that would become more important than his own presidency.

Photo courtesy of Franklin Roosevelt Library, NPx 63-536.

Eleanor and Franklin after their engagement announcement.

Promises Made
and
Broken

Chapter 4

1905 - 1918

Key Events in Eleanor Roosevelt's Life

Eleanor and Franklin are married on St. Patrick's Day. Her Uncle Teddy gives her away.

Anna Roosevelt, the first child of Eleanor and Franklin, is born on May 3.

James is born on December 23.

Franklin Jr. is born on March 18 and dies later in the year from influenza.

Elliott is born on September 23.

Eleanor attends her first Democratic Party convention, in Baltimore, Maryland.

The second Franklin Jr. is born on August 17.

John, the last child to be born to Eleanor and Franklin, is born on March 17, his parents' 11th wedding anniversary.

Eleanor volunteers to work for the Red Cross, visiting servicemen wounded in World War I.

Eleanor learns about Franklin's relationship with Lucy Mercer.

Key Events Around the World

Upton Sinclair describes the unhealthy practices of the meat packing industry in *The Jungle*. Congress passes the Pure Food and Drug Act.

The NAACP (National Association for the Advancement of Colored People) is organized in New York.

Jane Addams publishes *Twenty Years at Hull-House*.

Irving Berlin publishes his first hit song, *Alexander's Ragtime Band*.

The HMS *Titanic* collides with an iceberg and sinks. More than 1,000 passengers are lost at sea.

The Ford Motor Company makes a Model-T car in one hour, using an assembly line.

The Panama Canal opens to connect the Atlantic and Pacific Oceans.

V. I. Lenin leads a demonstration in Russia, beginning the Bolshevik Revolution.

Timeline years: 1905, 1906, 1907, 1909, 1910, 1911, 1912, 1913, 1914, 1915, 1916, 1917, 1918, 1920, 1925, 1930

*E*leanor and Franklin decided to get married in New York City on St. Patrick's Day—March 17, 1905—not because they were Irish, but because Teddy Roosevelt would be in town. As president of the United States, he planned to review the annual parade that marched up Fifth Avenue. By chance, the wedding was also on the birthday of Eleanor's mother, Anna Hall Roosevelt. Eleanor honored her mother's memory by covering her white satin wedding gown with the same Brussels lace that Anna and her own mother had worn. Some of the guests were startled by how much Eleanor looked like her mother.

As the ceremony started, the minister asked, "Who giveth this woman in marriage?" Eleanor's Uncle Ted boomed out, "*I* do!" When the minister pronounced the young couple man and wife, Uncle Ted congratulated Franklin on "keeping the name in the family."

During the party that followed the ceremony, Eleanor received a telegram from Mlle. Souvestre. It contained a single word: BONHEUR (Happiness). Two days later, Eleanor received another message—this time with the sad news that Mlle. Souvestre had died. Eleanor would have to chart her own course through life without the advice of her beloved mentor. As she thought about her new role as a married woman, Eleanor remarked: "I had . . . not the faintest notion of what it meant to be either a wife or a mother, and none of my elders enlightened me."

Photo courtesy of Franklin Roosevelt Library, NPx 73-182.51.

Eleanor on her wedding day, March 17, 1905.

Brussels lace:
A delicate lace with floral designs, made by hand in Brussels, Belgium.

Mentor:
A trusted person, often a teacher, who acts as a role model for a younger person.

Photo courtesy of Franklin Roosevelt Library, NPx 47-96-2388.

Photo courtesy of Franklin Roosevelt Library, NPx 47-96-4927(8).

Eleanor holding Franklin's hat, in a gondola in Venice on the last day of their honeymoon in 1905.

Top: Eleanor talking with Sara Roosevelt at Campobello in 1904.

A Life of Ease

Eleanor and Franklin began their life together at Springwood—the Roosevelt family home in Hyde Park. After Franklin completed his degree at Harvard, the couple left New York on a three-month honeymoon in Europe.

Italy brought back happy memories for Eleanor. As she rode in the gondolas of Venice, she could almost hear her father singing. She remembered the adventures she had while traveling with Mlle. Souvestre. Now Franklin took care of all the arrangements. Years later, she confided: "I was beginning to be an entirely dependent person. . . . A very pleasant contrast to my former life, and I slipped into it with the greatest of ease."

The couple returned home in September 1905—just in time to move into a new apartment. While they were in Europe, Sara had rented a townhouse for "her children" on East 36th Street—three blocks from her own house. She had also filled it with furniture and hired a cook, a butler, and a maid. As Franklin headed back to law school at Columbia University, Eleanor found herself overshadowed by Sara. "I was completely taken care of," recalled Eleanor. "My mother-in-law did everything for me." Soon, Sara would take over another area of their life.

A Growing Family

A short time after returning from Europe, Eleanor found out she was going to have a baby. She greeted the news with a mixture of joy and fear. She felt happy and relieved that she was able to have children. But she worried that the experiences of her own unhappy childhood would make her a poor mother. As her fears increased, her self-confidence began to crumble. She allowed the strong-willed Sara to take charge of every detail of daily life.

On May 3, 1906, Eleanor gave birth to a daughter, Anna Eleanor. On December 23, 1907, a son, James, followed. Sara decided that the growing family needed more room. She bought a plot of land and hired an architect to build two adjoining townhouses on East 65th Street.

Shortly after moving into her new six-story townhouse, Eleanor sat down at her dressing table and wept. When Franklin found her in tears, she told him that she did not like living in a house "which was not in any way mine." Franklin tried in vain to calm her. When Eleanor finally stopped crying, she realized:

> *I was not developing any individual taste. . . . I was simply absorbing the personalities of those about me and letting their tastes and interests dominate me.*

Eleanor's unhappiness deepened as her family grew. During the first five years of her marriage, she had four children—one girl and three boys. After Anna and James came Franklin Jr. and Elliott. As Eleanor put it, "I was always just getting over having a baby or about to have one." Sara made it her business to manage the children's care, prompting Eleanor to confess: "Franklin's children were more my mother-in-law's . . . than . . . mine." But when influenza claimed the life of seven-month-old Franklin Jr. in the fall of 1909, Eleanor blamed herself.

Franklin, Eleanor, Anna, and Sara at Hyde Park with Anna's pony, Daisy.

Top: Franklin, Eleanor, and their first child, Anna, in 1907.

Influenza:
A contagious virus that attacks the respiratory system; also known as "the flu."

New York State Senator
Franklin D. Roosevelt.

Top: The state capitol building in Albany,
New York.

She tried to escape her sadness, but she was living in a very confining world. She had given up her settlement house work. Nursemaids, hired by Sara, took care of the children. With little to do, Eleanor knitted, embroidered, read books, and took lessons in French, German, and Italian. She had little way of knowing that Franklin would soon open a door to a world much wider than any she had known.

Entering Public Life

When Franklin finished law school in 1907, he went to work for a successful law firm on Wall Street—the heart of New York's financial district. The work soon bored him. He dreamed of following in the political footsteps of Eleanor's Uncle Ted. On his journey to the White House, Uncle Ted had served as a state legislator, secretary of the navy, state governor, and vice president of the United States.

In 1910, Franklin got the chance to take the first step in that journey when Democratic leaders from the Hyde Park voting district asked him to run for the New York state senate. The Republican district had not elected a Democrat in 32 years. Nobody expected a 28-year-old New York City lawyer to win, but Democratic leaders felt Franklin had the wealth and the social connections to challenge the Republican candidate.

Eleanor was eager to support her husband's dreams. "I listened to all his plans with a great deal of interest," she later wrote. "It never occurred to me that I had any part to play."

Franklin won the election, and he and Eleanor headed to Albany, the capital of New York. For the first time in her marriage, Eleanor had a house of her own, and Sara could only visit. Eleanor later commented: "I had to stand on my own feet now, and I think I knew that it was good for me. . . . I was beginning to realize that something within me craved to be an individual."

The Political Wife

As Eleanor sat in the visitors' gallery in the state senate in Albany and heard debates on the issues of the day, she began to understand why politics so excited her husband. The debate that Eleanor most remembered concerned women's rights.

At that time, Eleanor knew little about the battles being waged by such woman suffrage leaders as Carrie Chapman Catt and Jane Addams. Eleanor was surprised when Franklin came out in favor of suffrage in 1911. She admitted she "had never given the question really serious thought" but decided "if my husband were a suffragist I . . . must be, too."

Eleanor was content to play the role of "political wife" in the 1912 elections that followed. She joined Franklin at the Democratic National Convention in Baltimore, Maryland, where Woodrow Wilson was nominated as the party's candidate for president. Eleanor declared herself a Democrat, despite the fact that her Uncle Ted had been a popular Republican president.

Shortly after his return from the Baltimore convention, Franklin enlisted Louis Howe—a brilliant reporter and campaign worker—to help with his campaign for reelection to the state senate. Eleanor was not

Woman Suffrage

In the mid-1800s, women began organizing to win the right to vote. Carrie Chapman Catt spent her life working for woman suffrage. Jane Addams, a leader in social reform for immigrants and women in the workplace, joined the battle for suffrage because she realized voting power could bring about change.

Above are Jane Addams (right) and Carrie Chapman Catt (left).

Carrie Chapman Catt photo courtesy of Library of Congress, LC-USZ62-12704.
Jane Addams photo courtesy of Library of Congress, LC-USZ62-95722.

Photo courtesy of Library of Congress, LC-USZ62-34095.

Photo courtesy of Franklin Roosevelt Library, NPx 59-85.

Woodrow Wilson with the outgoing president, Howard Taft, at the 1913 presidential inauguration.

Top: Louis Howe, Franklin Roosevelt's campaign manager and political adviser.

Neutrality:
A nation's decision not to participate on either side of a war or conflict.

U-boats:
German submarines used in World War I.

impressed with Howe, whom she thought, "looked like a troll out of a Catskill cave." Howe described himself as "one of the four ugliest men in [New York]," but he proved himself by taking over the campaign and guiding Franklin to victory in 1912.

Woodrow Wilson had also been victorious, claiming the presidency by a narrow margin. Franklin's earlier support of Wilson paid off; the president appointed him assistant secretary of the navy. Once again, Eleanor moved her family—this time to the nation's capital. Traveling close behind was the family of Louis Howe.

The Clouds of War

The Roosevelts arrived in Washington, D.C., at an extraordinary time in history. Europe was at war. Nation after nation lined up behind the Allies, led by Great Britain and France, or behind the Central Powers, which were dominated by Germany and Austria-Hungary. In 1914, Woodrow Wilson insisted on a policy of neutrality. Eleanor wrote of his position:

> *Woodrow Wilson . . . was determined that our nation should*
> *not be dragged into this war if it could possibly be kept out, . . .*
> *until the nation itself felt the urge to take a stand. . . .*

As the wife of the assistant secretary of the navy, Eleanor was busier than ever. In May 1915, German U-boats had sunk the British merchant ship *Lusitania*, killing almost 1,200 passengers. This aggressive use of submarine warfare on the Atlantic Ocean convinced Franklin that the United States must get involved in the war. He made it his business to travel widely and observe U.S. naval operations. In his absence, he asked Eleanor to take care of the family's social responsibilities.

Eleanor felt overwhelmed by the number of invitations and dinners, so she hired 22-year-old Lucy Mercer as her social secretary. Lucy, an attractive and lively young woman, soon became a family friend, often sharing meals with the Roosevelts. Lucy also managed Eleanor's office when Eleanor was away with the five children. In 1914 another Franklin Jr. was born, and John arrived in 1916. Eleanor and the children took frequent trips to Hyde Park or to the family's summer home on Campobello, an island off the coast of Maine.

The war was a constant threat. German U-boats in the Atlantic had now claimed three U.S. ships, turning American opinion against the Central Powers. In the spring of 1917, President Wilson delivered a Declaration of War to Congress. Franklin managed to get Eleanor a seat at Wilson's historic address. As Eleanor listened to the message, she felt "the world rocking around us." For the first time since the 1898 Spanish-American War, American troops left the United States to fight in an overseas war. World War I, called the Great War, was the first of two global wars in which Eleanor and Franklin Roosevelt would play a key part.

Battles at Home and Abroad

Preparations for war turned life upside down in Washington, D.C. As Franklin worked to mobilize the U.S. Navy, Eleanor supported the American Red Cross, working at a tin-roofed canteen set up in Union Station in Washington, D.C. She served soup, coffee, and sandwiches to soldiers boarding troop trains.

Photo courtesy of Library of Congress, LC-USZ62-21728.

The sinking of the *Lusitania*.

Central Powers:

The Central Powers fought against the Allies in World War I. They included Germany, Austria-Hungary, Bulgaria, and Turkey.

Declaration of War:

A formal announcement by one country of the intent to go to war with another country.

Mobilize:

To assemble or prepare troops for battle.

Canteen:

A location that provides food and entertainment for soldiers.

Photo courtesy of FDR National Archives, 66-G23L-239.

Pennsylvania Avenue in
Washington, D.C., in 1915.

Double pneumonia:
An acute, or severe, bacterial infection that
inflames both lungs.

Photo courtesy of CORBIS/Bettmann, UPI 117830.

John and Franklin Jr. with their mother
around 1919, just after the discovery of
the Lucy Mercer letters.

In addition to her work at the canteen, Eleanor visited military hospitals. Wearing a Red Cross uniform, she spent time with wounded and shell-shocked soldiers—young men who had suffered emotional stress under the constant barrage of exploding shells. She watched with fear and pride as her cousins and her brother, Hall, marched off to war. And she supported Franklin's decision to travel overseas for the Department of the Navy. He planned to spend several months touring naval bases and visiting the war front.

In Franklin's absence, Eleanor stayed busy with her Red Cross work. On September 12, 1918, two months after Franklin's departure, Eleanor received a telegram from Europe urging her to bring an ambulance and doctors to meet Franklin's ship in New York harbor. Franklin had double pneumonia and had to be carried off the ship on a stretcher.

As fever raged through Franklin's body, Eleanor unpacked his bag. Near the bottom of the bag, she found a stack of letters in a neat bundle. She recognized the handwriting immediately. They were love letters written to Franklin by Lucy Mercer! Years later, Eleanor described the shattering effect of her discovery:

> *The bottom dropped out of my particular world & I faced*
> *myself, my surroundings, my world, honestly for the first time.*
> *I really grew up that year. . . .*

Finding

Her Way

Chapter 5

1918 - 1921

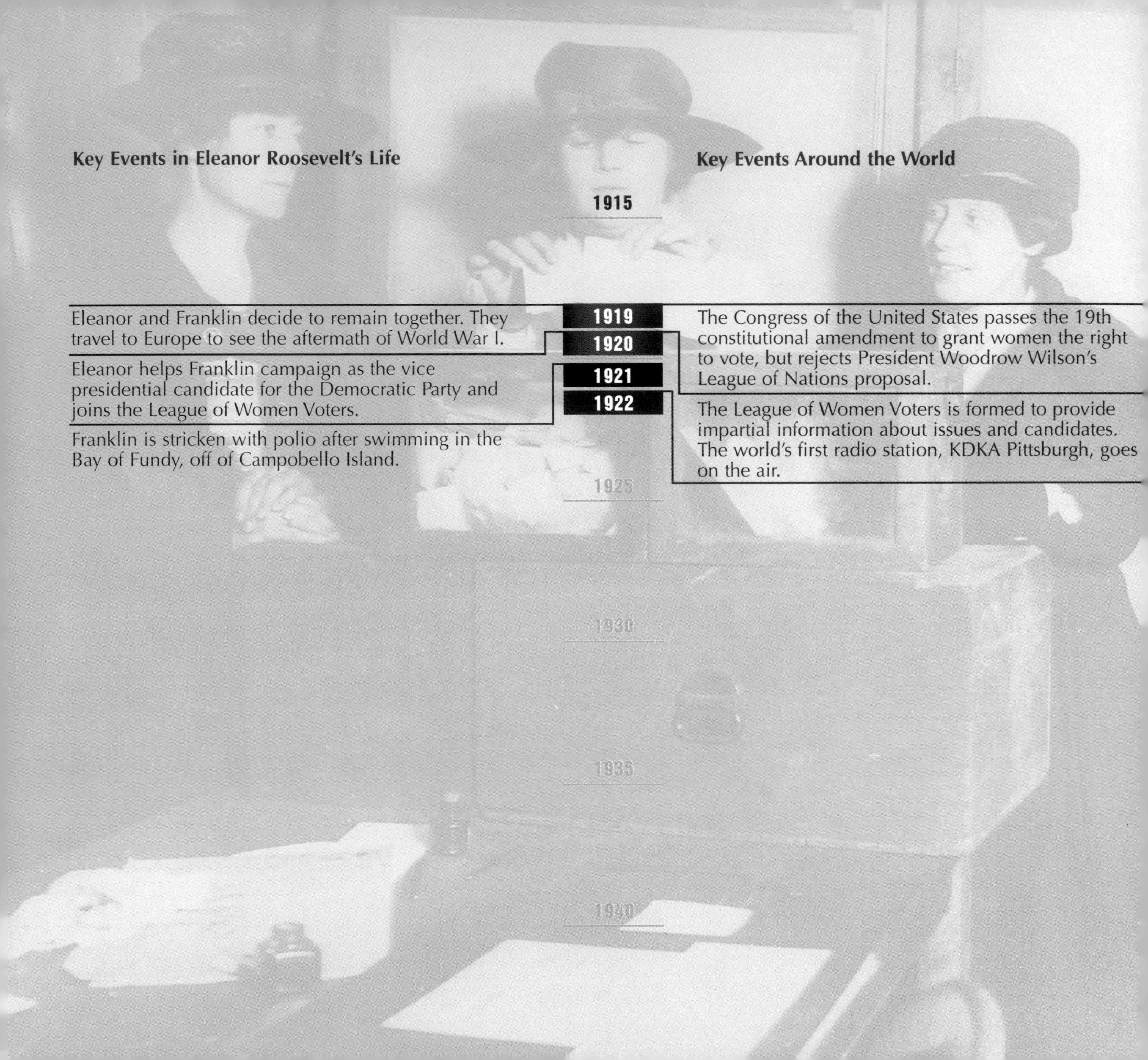

Key Events in Eleanor Roosevelt's Life

Key Events Around the World

1915

1919 Eleanor and Franklin decide to remain together. They travel to Europe to see the aftermath of World War I.

1920 Eleanor helps Franklin campaign as the vice presidential candidate for the Democratic Party and joins the League of Women Voters.

1921 Franklin is stricken with polio after swimming in the Bay of Fundy, off of Campobello Island.

1922

The Congress of the United States passes the 19th constitutional amendment to grant women the right to vote, but rejects President Woodrow Wilson's League of Nations proposal.

The League of Women Voters is formed to provide impartial information about issues and candidates. The world's first radio station, KDKA Pittsburgh, goes on the air.

1925

1930

1935

1940

$\mathcal{E}$leanor felt betrayed by Franklin. After 13 years of marriage and six children, he had fallen in love with someone else. Eleanor told her husband that she would grant him a divorce, but she advised Franklin: "Take time to think things over carefully."

Divorce would carry a heavy price for Franklin. Not only would he lose his wife and children, for whom he cared deeply, he would also lose his inheritance. Sara threatened to cut him off completely if he left Eleanor for another woman.

Any hint of scandal also promised to end Franklin's political career. Louis Howe tried to persuade the couple to patch up their marriage. He urged Franklin to remember his political dreams. He told Eleanor that she could help Franklin reach his goals and that she, too, had a great role to play. He also asked her to consider the children.

In the end, Eleanor and Franklin agreed to remain married. Years later, the couple's daughter, Anna, described the compromise reached by her parents: "He voluntarily promised to end any 'romantic relationship' with Lucy and seemed to realize how much pain he had given [my mother]." Eleanor, in turn, promised to stay at Franklin's side—at least in public. In private, she wanted a life separate from his.

Franklin, Sara, Eleanor, and the five Roosevelt children, with their dog, Chief, at Campobello in 1920.

Photo courtesy of Franklin Roosevelt Library, NPx 60-5.

Photo courtesy of National Archives, 104.111-SC-94980.

World War I battle scene.

Eleanor healed slowly. "I have the memory of an elephant," she confided to a friend. "I can forgive, but I cannot forget." No longer would Eleanor anchor her hopes and dreams to Franklin. As her son Elliott later wrote:

> The seed of independence began to . . . [grow], I believe, when Mother learned of Father's original involvement with Lucy. . . . she started . . . to create a separate existence for herself, "to use my own mind and abilities for my own aims," as she put it.

Planning for Peace

On January 1, 1919, Eleanor moved into the political spotlight when she accompanied Franklin on a trip to Europe. The Great War had come to a close with the signing of the armistice on November 11, 1918. Although the Allies had won the war, much work remained to be done, and Franklin wanted to be part of that work. He asked the secretary of the navy, Josephus Daniels, to send him back to Europe to help close down U.S. naval bases.

Eleanor and Franklin traveled to Europe at a key point in history. The trip coincided with the Paris Peace Conference—the meeting where President Wilson and other Allied leaders would work out the terms of peace. The war had claimed the lives of more than 9 million soldiers and left another 22 million wounded. Much of Europe lay in ruins. Many nations now looked to the United States for leadership.

Armistice:

An agreement between warring nations to cease fighting and establish terms for keeping the peace.

Allied:

The group of mostly European countries that joined together against the Central Powers during World War I and against the Axis powers in World War II. The United States eventually joined the Allied forces in both wars.

Eleanor's Uncle Ted had hoped to play a part in building world peace after the war. Unfortunately, he never got that opportunity. While Eleanor and Franklin were on their way to Europe, Theodore Roosevelt died. When she heard over the ship radio of her uncle's death, Eleanor spoke of the national loss: "I realized . . . that a great personality had gone from active participation in the life of his people." Eleanor, like many other people around the world, now placed her hopes in President Wilson. He wanted a "just and lasting peace" that would end war forever.

As Eleanor toured Europe, she got a firsthand look at the brutal effects of war. In Paris, she saw women dressed in black, mourning the losses of war. In war hospitals, she felt stunned at the sight of so many wounded soldiers. Out in the countryside, she glimpsed the battlefields on which some of these soldiers had fallen. Describing the destruction, Eleanor wrote:

> *We drove along the straight military roads with churned mud on either side of us, and deep shell holes here and there. Along the road there were occasional piles of stones with a stick stuck into them with the name of a vanished village. On the hillsides occasional stumps showed that once there had been a forest. . . .*

Eleanor's tour left her with a lasting hatred for war. As she prepared to return home, a reporter gave her a copy of Wilson's plan for an international peacekeeping organization called the League of Nations.

A World War I makeshift hospital in a bombed-out church.

The facade of the League of Nations headquarters in Geneva, Switzerland, October 1920.

League of Nations:
An association of nations formed by President Woodrow Wilson following World War I for the purpose of settling world conflicts by negotiation rather than with military force.

Photo courtesy of Library of Congress, LC-USZ62-31799

Isolationists:
Those who believed the United States should not become involved in the disputes and affairs of other nations.

Women suffragists picketing in front of the White House in February 1917.

Communism:
Russian Communism, although based on the 19th-century ideas of Karl Marx, resulted from the 1917 Bolshevik Revolution, led by Vladimir Lenin. In this system, the state would own everything, until workers could take over production.

The president had included his plan in the Treaty of Versailles, the agreement officially ending the war. Eleanor later recalled her reaction to Wilson's peace plan: "What hopes we had that this League would really prove [to be] the instrument for the prevention of future wars . . . !"

Eleanor knew from newspaper reports that not all Americans shared the president's faith in the League. After the horrors of battle, many people, including Eleanor's outspoken cousin Alice, were becoming isolationists. They wanted to stay out of world affairs.

Opinions in Turmoil

Eleanor returned home to a nation in turmoil. A bitter debate erupted over whether the United States should join the League of Nations. But the League was not the only issue dividing Americans in 1919. The war, which had been fought to "make the world safe for democracy," inspired those who still lacked the full benefits of American citizenship to speak out for equality. Woman suffrage leaders pointed to the contributions of women during the war and made their demands for the vote louder than ever. African Americans, who had fought for freedom abroad, now battled against inequality at home.

Factory workers, whose labor had fueled war-related industries, took part in more than 3,300 strikes for improved pay, better working conditions, and the right to organize unions. Labor leaders were often charged with spreading Communism. When Attorney General A. Mitchell Palmer launched a widespread investigation to track down Communists in the

United States, he set off a "Red Scare." Americans were afraid that a revolt similar to the 1917 Russian Revolution would erupt in the United States. The Red Scare investigation falsely accused many American citizens of being Communists.

Eleanor felt the effects of these turbulent events firsthand. The Anti-Suffrage Society asked her to join them, but she refused. In the summer of 1919, race riots shook Washington, D.C., and Eleanor feared for the safety of her family. A short time later, a bomb exploded in front of A. Mitchell Palmer's house, blowing out the front windows in the Roosevelt home across the street. As waves of protest jolted the nation, Eleanor began to see reform as the only way to avoid a political revolution.

At this time, Eleanor was also facing many personal changes. She lost several family members in a short span of time. Both her Grandmother Hall and Aunt Edith Hall died shortly after Uncle Ted. Still in pain from the Lucy Mercer affair, Eleanor sometimes lost patience with Franklin. She found herself more and more on her own, thinking for herself and speaking out—to Franklin, to Sara, to the world.

She took a stand in favor of the United States' membership in the League of Nations—the leading issue in the upcoming presidential election. In 1920, after spending time with Sara and her two sisters, she wrote to Franklin: "[Their] absolute judgments on people and affairs going on in the world . . . make me want to squirm and turn bolshevik." Eleanor was becoming a rebel!

Red Scare:
Two periods in American history when the government conducted investigations of private citizens, believing that Russian Communists (nicknamed Reds) were secretly recruiting U.S. citizens.

Men studying issues at the national Anti-Suffrage Society headquarters.

Eleanor was an active campaigner in the 1920 elections.

Supporters gather to congratulate Franklin when he is nominated for vice president in 1920, among them Josephus Daniels and New York governor Al Smith.

Campaigning for Progress

Soon, Eleanor was involved in campaigning for the 1920 elections. Franklin had resigned from the Navy Department to enter national politics. At the Democratic National Convention, he supported the nomination of Ohio governor James M. Cox as the party's candidate for president. Cox repaid the favor by picking Franklin as his running mate. With the passage of the 19th Amendment to the Constitution in 1920, women would be voting for the first time in the upcoming election. Franklin wanted Eleanor at his side on the campaign trail, because he believed a visible candidate's wife could help bring women voters to the polls.

Franklin viewed his candidacy for vice president as a chance to introduce himself to the nation. Dreaming of a future run for the presidency, he embarked on a train ride across the United States, insisting that Eleanor travel with him. As Franklin gave speeches, Eleanor smiled, took notes, or yanked his coattails if he talked too long.

As the only woman among a group of male politicians and reporters, Eleanor felt like an outsider. Franklin spent most nights in a smoke-filled railroad car, planning the next day's strategy. Louis Howe sensed Eleanor's loneliness and tried to make her feel part of the campaign. He explained his plans for Franklin and sought her advice. "I was flattered[,] and before long I found myself discussing a wide range of subjects," recalled Eleanor. By the end of the trip, Louis and Eleanor had formed a lasting friendship.

From the start, Eleanor predicted a Republican victory. Senator Henry Cabot Lodge led Republican senators to block passage of Wilson's peace plan, including membership in the League of Nations. The Republican candidate for president, Warren G. Harding, promised voters a "return to normalcy." Tired of war and protests, voters handed Harding an overwhelming victory. After 10 years in the political spotlight, Eleanor and Franklin returned to private life and moved the family back to New York.

A Self-Improvement Program

Eleanor emerged from the 1920 election campaign with a new sense of independence. "I did not look forward to . . . [having] nothing but teas and luncheons . . . to take up my time," she explained.

Franklin took a job with a private law firm, and Eleanor went to business school. She took courses in typing and shorthand because she wanted to be able to earn her own money. She tried to learn to cook but found she could cook only scrambled eggs and hot dogs. She served these two dishes to guests for the rest of her life.

Besides taking courses, Eleanor joined the League of Women Voters. Narcissa Vanderlip, the chairman of the New York branch of the League, asked Eleanor to serve on its legislative committee. Her job was to report on national laws. When Eleanor doubted her own ability, Narcissa promised her the help of a lawyer named Elizabeth Read. "I felt very humble and inadequate . . . when I presented myself to Elizabeth Read," recalled Eleanor, "but I liked her at once and she gave me a sense of confidence."

Photo courtesy of Library of Congress, LC-USZ62-38504 neg#16421.

Photo courtesy of Library of Congress, LC-USZ62-106244.

President Warren Harding.

Top: Senator Henry Cabot Lodge.

League of Women Voters:
Founded in 1920 by veterans of the battle for woman suffrage, the League worked to educate women about the workings of the U.S. government.

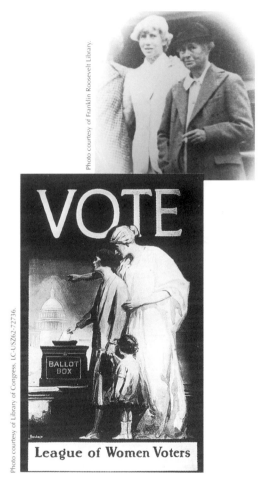

Photo courtesy of Franklin Roosevelt Library.

Photo courtesy of Library of Congress. LC-USZ62-72736.

A poster for the League of Women Voters from around 1920.

Top: Esther Lape and Elizabeth Read.

Eleanor's confidence continued to grow as she met others in the League of Women Voters. She formed a lifelong friendship with Elizabeth and her roommate, Esther Lape, a college professor and writer. Eleanor credited her new friends with what she called "the intensive education of Eleanor Roosevelt." She was at last becoming the independent thinker that Mlle. Souvestre had encouraged at Allenswood.

Eleanor worried about how her new activities might affect Franklin's political career. But concerns for his future did not silence her views on important issues. She continued to support the League of Nations until 1921, when the Senate firmly rejected it and negotiated a separate peace treaty with Germany. She also openly opposed the excesses of the Red Scare. Eleanor's outspoken opinions were silenced only by the personal tragedy that almost ended Franklin's political career.

The Ultimate Challenge

In the summer of 1921, the Roosevelt family took their usual vacation on Campobello Island. On August 10, after a long day of deep-sea fishing, Franklin jumped into the cold waters of the Bay of Fundy. He then ran home and sat on the windswept porch in his wet bathing suit. About 4 p.m., Franklin complained of a chill and went to bed.

Franklin's condition quickly worsened. On August 14, which was the anniversary of her father's death, Eleanor wrote about Franklin's illness for the first time. In a letter to one of his relatives, she shared alarming news:

> We have had a very anxious few days[,] as on Wed. evening
> Franklin was taken ill. It seemed a chill[,] but Thursday he had
> so much pain in his back and legs that I sent for the doctor, [and]
> by Friday evening, he lost the ability to walk or move his legs.

Doctors puzzled over the cause of Franklin's ailment. Eleanor finally called in a specialist from Newport, Rhode Island. After examining Franklin, he told Eleanor that her 39-year-old husband might never walk again. Franklin suffered from infantile paralysis—also known as polio. There was no vaccination against polio at the time, and no known cure. Was his public life over? His mother, Sara, thought so. But two other people—Louis Howe and Eleanor Roosevelt—thought otherwise. They decided to fight for Franklin's future at a time when he was too weak to fight for it himself.

Polio

This 3,000-year-old Egyptian stone slab shows evidence of the crippling effects of polio in ancient times. Polio was a widespread disease until the early 1950s, when a medicine (vaccine) was developed by Dr. Jonas Salk that could protect people from the disease.

Photo courtesy of the March of Dimes.

Photo courtesy of Franklin Roosevelt Library, NPx 47-96-4863, and CORBIS/Bettmann.

Photo courtesy of Franklin Roosevelt Library, NPx 47-96-2431.

A Roosevelt family picnic at Campobello
Island, August 1913.

Top: The Roosevelt house at Campobello,
off the coast of Maine.

A

Passion

for

Politics

Chapter 6

1921 - 1924

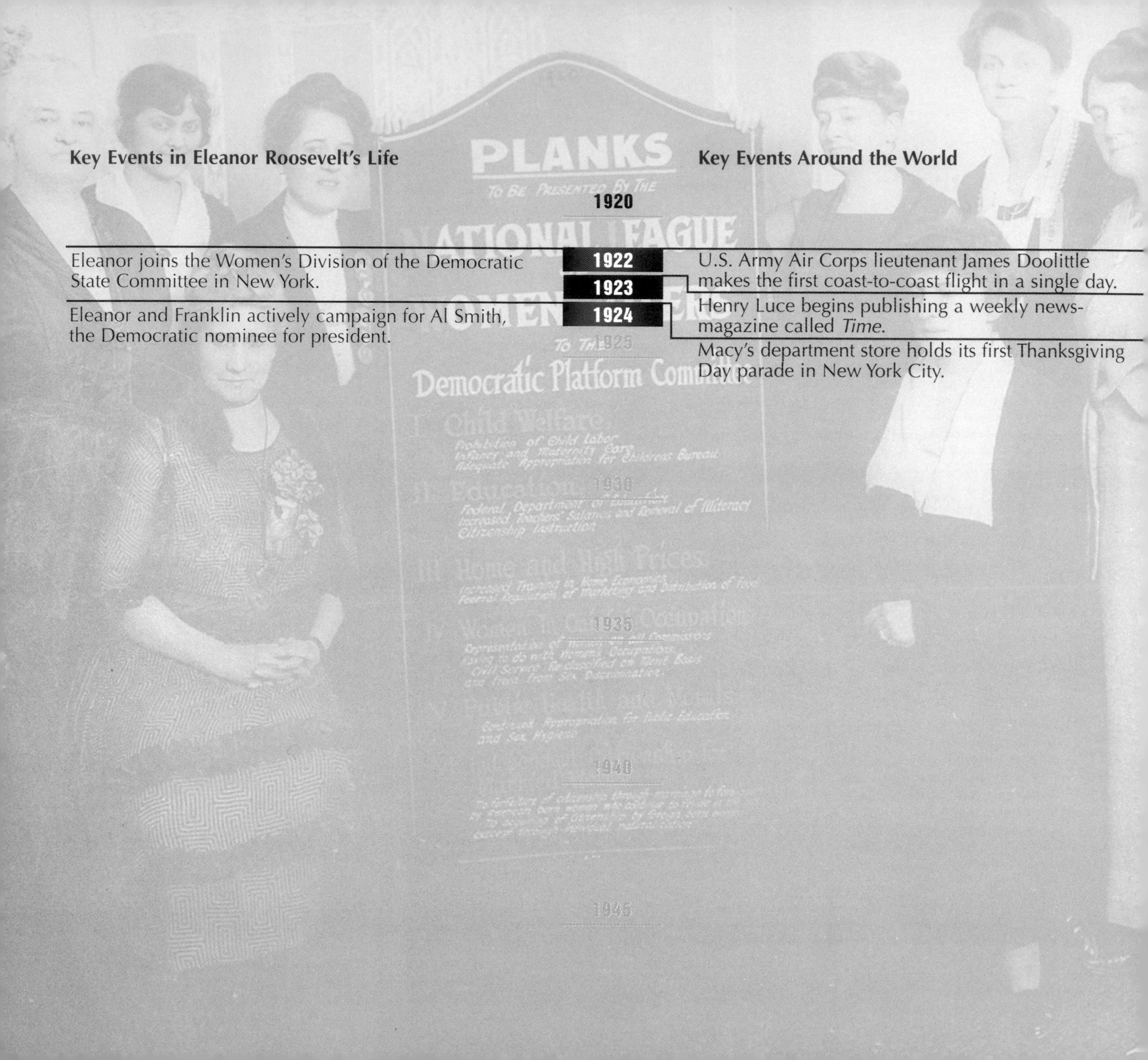

Key Events in Eleanor Roosevelt's Life | **Key Events Around the World**

1920

1922
Eleanor joins the Women's Division of the Democratic State Committee in New York.
U.S. Army Air Corps lieutenant James Doolittle makes the first coast-to-coast flight in a single day.

1923
Henry Luce begins publishing a weekly newsmagazine called *Time*.

1924
Eleanor and Franklin actively campaign for Al Smith, the Democratic nominee for president.
Macy's department store holds its first Thanksgiving Day parade in New York City.

1925

1930

1935

1940

1945

During the first three weeks of Franklin's crippling illness, Eleanor slept on a small couch in his room and waited on him day and night. When Franklin's arms were temporarily paralyzed, she fed him, brushed his teeth, bathed him, and, most important, kept up his spirits. Neither Franklin nor Eleanor complained. They even joked at times.

In September 1921, Eleanor moved Franklin from Campobello Island to a special hospital in New York City. Strapped to a stretcher, Franklin traveled by car, boat, train, and ambulance. Each bump or jolt sent a wave of pain through his body. The trip was made bearable by one thought—recovery.

Two months after Franklin entered the hospital, the doctors sent him home—still in pain and unable to move his legs. Eleanor decided that the family should return to their townhouse on East 65th Street, where Franklin could carry on his "various business activities." She invited Louis Howe to move into one of the bedrooms so that he could help Franklin rebuild his life. With Louis at her side, Eleanor began what she described as "the most trying winter of my entire life."

Eleanor and Sara engaged in a battle of wills over Franklin's future. Sara thought Franklin should retire and live out his life as an invalid. To get back at Eleanor for disagreeing with her, Sara used Louis as a wedge between Eleanor and her children. Fifteen-year-old Anna was already angry with Eleanor for sending her to a strict New York City girls' school. Sara added fuel to that anger by convincing Anna that Eleanor cared more for Louis than for her own daughter. Eleanor now had to deal with a bedridden husband and a rebellious teenager who was jealous of Louis.

Photo courtesy of Franklin Roosevelt Library, NPx 48-65(1).

Three years after he became ill with polio, Franklin was able to stand only with the help of others.

Photo courtesy of Franklin Roosevelt Library, NPx 81-91(542).

Eleanor and Anna, playfully wrestling at Val-Kill, July 1925.

Tears and Triumph

In April 1922, Eleanor finally broke down. While reading to five-year-old John and seven-year-old Franklin Jr., she started crying. "I could not think why I was sobbing," explained Eleanor, "nor could I stop." The children were disturbed at the sight of their mother weeping. Eventually, Eleanor choked back the tears and carried on. "From that time on I seemed to have got rid of nerves and uncontrollable tears," Eleanor recalled.

She observed that "the effect . . . was rather good on Anna." A short time later, Anna broke down in tears, too. She blurted out stories of bad experiences at her school and confessed her jealousy of Louis. Eleanor assured Anna of her love. Then, as Anna recalled: "Mother told me of the battle Father was waging against great odds. . . ."

Coping with Franklin's illness brought mother and daughter closer together and freed Eleanor from Sara once and for all. Eleanor believed that if she had given in to Sara, she would have "stayed a weak character forever." Instead, she was ready to "stand on my own two feet." Louis showed Eleanor the direction in which she should walk. With Franklin sidelined by polio, Louis urged Eleanor to keep the Roosevelt name alive by jumping into politics herself.

On the Move

Eleanor stepped cautiously into the political arena. "I'm only being *active* till you can be again," she assured Franklin. Within a year, however, Eleanor had found her purpose in life. As her son James later wrote, she became "filled with a passion for politics through which she saw the chance to right wrongs, to be of use."

In 1922, Eleanor joined the Women's Trade Union League (WTUL) and met Rose Schneiderman. Eleanor never forgot the horrible sweatshops she had visited while working with the Consumers' League as a 19-year-old volunteer. At age 37, Eleanor wanted to improve the conditions of working women everywhere.

Eleanor turned to Rose Schneiderman for guidance. The two women seemed unlikely friends. Eleanor's family history stretched back to the first Dutch settlers of New York. Rose was a working-class woman who had traveled to the United States from Russian Poland in 1891. Despite their differences, Eleanor and Rose shared an important goal—to protect women workers.

One Sunday night in 1922, Eleanor invited Rose to supper. Eleanor served scrambled eggs and coffee. Rose liked Eleanor's "simplicity"— and her interest in raising money for a new WTUL headquarters. Rose later recalled the evening: "We talked about the work I was doing. . . . [S]he was particularly interested in why I thought women should join unions."

Women's Trade Union League (WTUL):
An organization formed in Chicago in 1903 to protect wage-earning women by promoting an eight-hour workday, a minimum wage, an end to child labor, and the right to form unions.

The seal of the national Women's Trade Union League.

Top: Rose Schneiderman.

Photo courtesy of Library of Congress, Lot 5793G.

Maud Swartz of the
national Women's Trade Union League.

Minimum wage:
A policy set by the U.S. government setting
the lowest wage a worker could be paid.

The meeting cemented their friendship. Rose introduced Eleanor to Maud Swartz, president of the WTUL. Eleanor took the bold step of inviting the two women to Hyde Park, and later to Campobello. She knew her mother-in-law would not approve. Eleanor introduced Rose and Maud to Franklin, and they gave him his first inside look at the labor movement. They spent hours describing the struggle of working 14-hour days—often at the risk of life and limb—only to remain on the edge of poverty. Later, when Franklin came out in favor of unions, a labor leader remarked: "You'd almost think he had participated in some strike . . . the way he knew and felt about it."

Through the League of Women Voters, Eleanor supported laws that furthered the goals of the WTUL—a 48-hour workweek, an end to child labor, a minimum wage, and the right to form unions. A few years later, inspired by the women of the WTUL, Eleanor shocked her well-to-do friends by joining more than 300 striking paper-box makers as they marched through the streets of the Lower West Side of New York City.

Trooping for Democracy

The same year that Eleanor joined the WTUL, she met Marion Dickerman and Nancy Cook. In 1920, Marion had run for the state assembly—the first woman to seek legislative office in New York. Nancy was her campaign manager. Although Marion lost the election, the two women remained active in politics and helped to organize the women's division of the New York State Democratic Party. Nancy asked Eleanor to join them—a request enthusiastically supported by Louis Howe.

Marion and Nancy introduced Eleanor to their co-workers, Caroline O'Day and Elinor Morgenthau. The five women bought a bright blue touring car and went "Trooping for Democracy." Rain or shine, they traveled all over New York State working for a wide range of issues. They asked women voters to demand new parks and playgrounds, school lunch programs, and laws requiring children to attend public school. They also lobbied for fair labor laws and rights for women, including the right to equal representation on all committees in the Democratic Party.

Eleanor did not mind talking to people face to face, but she feared speaking in front of a large audience. She clung to her notes, giggled nervously, and talked in a high-pitched, squeaky voice. Louis stepped in to coach Eleanor. He edited her speeches and then watched her deliver them. He told Eleanor to look the audience in the eye and "Have something you want to say, say it and sit down."

Eleanor used her speeches to fire away at the Republican candidates. In the 1922 election for New York State governor, she urged voters to look to the future and vote for the Democratic candidate, Al Smith. At the state Democratic convention in August, Eleanor led a delegate parade for Al Smith. On election day, she offered rides to any man or woman who wanted to cast a ballot for Al Smith.

Lobbied:

Influenced public officials or lawmakers to pass legislation favoring a particular cause.

Photo courtesy of Franklin Roosevelt Library, NPx 81-91/490.

Eleanor with her friends Marion Dickerman (far left), Nancy Cook (second from right), and Marion's sister, Peggy Levenson, in front of one of their touring cars.

Photo courtesy of Library of Congress, LC-USZ62-12538/neg 136443/lot 43941).

Edward W. Bok.

World Court:

An international judicial body established by the League of Nations in 1920 for the purpose of settling disputes between countries.

Photo courtesy of Franklin Roosevelt Library, NPx 72-170.

Eleanor Roosevelt and Esther Lape, entering the U.S. Capitol to appear before a congressional committee investigating their involvement in the American Peace Award, in 1924.

Women for Peace

Al Smith was elected governor of New York by a landslide. Shortly after the campaign, a new project came to Eleanor's attention. Her friend Esther Lape asked her to help pick the winner of the American Peace Award—a nationwide contest for the most feasible plan by which the United States could cooperate with other nations to achieve and preserve world peace.

Edward W. Bok, the former editor and publisher of the *Ladies' Home Journal*, sponsored the contest. Bok offered $50,000 to the person who came up with the winning plan. The contest made headline news. A total of 22,165 entries poured into the committee. Even Franklin worked on a plan, which he called the Society of Nations. Although he did not submit it, the plan helped shape Franklin's thinking on international cooperation. In the end, the committee picked a simple plan by Charles E. Levermore, who suggested that the United States join the World Court and cooperate with the League of Nations.

The contest set off a firestorm of debate. Isolationists, who had opposed U.S. entry into the League of Nations, charged that the contest had been staged to influence public opinion in favor of the League. They branded the contest "un-American" and demanded a Senate investigation. At hearings held in January 1924, Esther Lape defended herself and praised the contributions of Eleanor Roosevelt.

The hearings were suspended when former president Woodrow Wilson died on February 3, 1924. Although the hearings never resumed, the Federal Bureau of Investigation (FBI) opened a file on Eleanor. The first entry linked Eleanor to the American Peace Award.

Eleanor continued to defend the idea of international cooperation for peace. With the help of Louis, Eleanor drafted a widely quoted speech in which she called on women to fight for U.S. participation in the World Court. In stirring words, she asked:

> *Cannot the women rise to this great opportunity and work*
> *now, and not have the double horror, if another war comes, of*
> *losing their loved ones, and knowing that they lifted no finger*
> *when they might have worked hard?*

With this question Eleanor joined the debate over the World Court that raged until 1935, when the Senate officially rejected U.S. membership. By that time, Eleanor and Franklin—who were champions of international cooperation—were in the White House.

Eleanor Roosevelt with other members of the Peace Award committee, Mrs. Frank Vanderlip (Narcissa) and Mrs. Gifford Pinchot, in 1923.

Sharing the Spotlight

Franklin found it difficult to surrender the political spotlight to Eleanor. He worked hard to be able to walk again. "Little by little, through exercise and wearing braces," wrote Eleanor, "he learned to walk, first with crutches and then with a cane, leaning on someone's arm." As the 1924 presidential election neared, both Roosevelts took center stage.

Once again, Eleanor mobilized the women's division of the New York State Democratic Party. This time, the committee would champion Franklin's nomination of Governor Al Smith as the Democratic candidate for president.

Al Smith in 1925.

Photo courtesy of Franklin Roosevelt Library, NPx 63-488.

Eleanor Roosevelt, Nancy Cook, Caroline O'Day, and Marion Dickerman at Democratic State Committee Headquarters.

Platform:

A declared position adopted by a political candidate or party.

Eleanor demanded that members of the women's division be given the right to help name delegates to the Democratic National Convention. Some male members balked at the idea, but Eleanor fought back by rallying women voters. "Get into the game and stay in it," she urged. At a women's dinner in Albany, she declared:

> *To many women, and I am one of them, it is extraordinarily difficult to care about anything enough to cause disagreement . . . , but I have come to the conclusion that this must be done for a time. . . . We will be strengthened if we can show that we are willing to fight to the very last ditch for what we believe in.*

A front-page story of the *New York Times* proclaimed:

WOMEN ARE IN REVOLT!

Governor Al Smith quieted the revolt by persuading party leaders to accept the women's demands. Eleanor told reporters: "No better evidence could be shown that it is to the Democratic Party that the women voters of this State must turn."

That summer, Eleanor marched off to the national convention as part of a special women's committee to work on the Democratic platform. Eleanor immediately ran into opposition. Her handpicked committee found itself locked out of all-male meetings that refused to hear the women's proposals. Eleanor later wrote:

I [saw] for the first time where the women stood when it came to a national convention. I shortly discovered that they were of very little importance. They stood outside the door of all important meetings and waited.

Eleanor believed it was critical that Governor Smith, who had supported women, receive the Democratic nomination. She looked on with pride as Franklin stood up to place Smith's name before the convention. Franklin, who had once leaped over a row of seats to address the 1920 convention, now struggled down the aisle to reach the speaker's platform.

With sweat beading on his brow, he dragged his heavily braced legs forward. He worked a crutch with one arm and leaned on his 16-year-old son, James, with the other arm. When they reached the platform, James handed Franklin a second crutch and watched his father pull himself onto the stage. Alone in the spotlight, Franklin walked stiffly to the podium. He gripped each side and let the crutches fall. He then tipped back his head, flashed his trademark grin, and listened as the crowd erupted into cheers.

Franklin quieted the hall with his booming, eloquent voice. He asked delegates to elect Al Smith, "the Happy Warrior of the political battlefield," as their candidate for president. When he finished speaking, delegates stomped, shouted, and applauded for an hour and 13 minutes. In the end, the ballot went to West Virginia Democrat John W. Davis. But nobody forgot Franklin's impact. Both the Democrats and the press called him the true "Happy Warrior" of the 1924 convention. The nickname stuck.

Franklin nominates Al Smith for president at the Democratic National Convention in 1924.

Photo courtesy of Library of Congress, LC-USZ62-36747.

Josephus Daniels.

Eleanor and Franklin returned home to resume their political partnership. While Franklin worked behind the scenes, Eleanor threw herself into the campaign to reelect Al Smith as governor. Franklin jokingly told his longtime friend Josephus Daniels that he had a new plan: He would keep his name out of the newspapers for three years while Eleanor grabbed the headlines. "Each fourth year (Presidential ones)," explained Franklin, "I am to have all the limelight." Franklin told Daniels that he felt sure his plan would win him a slot on the Democratic ticket in either 1928 or 1932. Eleanor, who rarely joked about anything, put Franklin's plan into effect by making headline news almost as soon as she got back to Hyde Park.

The *Political* Partnership

Chapter 7

1924 - 1932

Key Events in Eleanor Roosevelt's Life

Key Events Around the World

1920

A. Philip Randolph organizes the Sleeping Car Porters Union and begins publishing *The Messenger.* The Ku Klux Klan stages a large demonstration in Washington, D.C.

1924

Franklin first visits Warm Springs, Georgia, which he later helps turn into a treatment center for polio victims.

A. A. Milne introduces *Winnie-the-Pooh.* Joseph Stalin becomes dictator of the Union of Soviet Socialist Republics (USSR).

1925

1926

Eleanor and Franklin build Val-Kill Cottage near the Roosevelt family home at Hyde Park, New York.

Charles A. Lindbergh flies the *Spirit of St. Louis* solo across the Atlantic Ocean and becomes an international hero.

1927

Eleanor purchases the Todhunter School with her friends Marion Dickerman and Nancy Cook.

1928

1929

Walt Disney introduces Mickey Mouse in the cartoon "Steamboat Willie."

Eleanor helps with Al Smith's presidential campaign, while Franklin runs for governor of New York.

1930

The New York stock market crash of October 29 marks the beginning of the Great Depression.

1931

Eleanor visits bread lines and soup kitchens, listening to the problems of Americans hit hard by the Great Depression.

The Continental Baking Company introduces sliced Wonder Bread and Twinkies.

1932

The Star Spangled Banner becomes the official national anthem.

1935

A "Bonus Army" of 25,000 poor World War I veterans invade Washington, D.C., and demand "a promised bonus" for wartime service.

1940

1945

The family of former president Teddy Roosevelt saw Eleanor and Franklin as traitors. True Roosevelts, they claimed, would never become Democrats! The Roosevelt family should support the Republicans, the party that had sent Teddy to the White House.

Insults hurled at Franklin from the Teddy Roosevelt clan during the 1920 campaign had angered him: "This is one thing . . . at least some members of the Roosevelt family will not forget."

The honor of defending the family's name fell to Eleanor. When Theodore Roosevelt's son (TR Jr.) challenged Al Smith for the office of New York governor in 1924, Eleanor devised a campaign strategy to oppose him. She took advantage of a scandal during Republican president Warren G. Harding's administration. One of his officials had received kickbacks for leasing oil-rich government lands in Teapot Dome, Wyoming, to a private oil company. Although TR Jr. had nothing to do with the Teapot Dome scandal, Eleanor made sure he spent most of his time proving it.

Eleanor and Louis Howe put a giant steam-spouting teapot on top of a car that followed TR Jr. wherever he went. In speech after speech, Eleanor dismissed him as "a personally nice young man whose public service record shows him willing to do the bidding of his friends." Eleanor called the tactic a "rough stunt," but she was delighted when TR Jr. lost by a landslide.

Jessie Tarbox Beals photo courtesy of Franklin Roosevelt Library, NPx 58-348.

Louis Howe, across from Eleanor, at a Democratic Party meeting for Governor Al Smith in 1924.

Kickbacks:
Secret payments received by a person in return for helping a business or organization win a contract.

Teapot Dome scandal:
An incident of government corruption in the early 1920s; federally owned oil reserve lands in Teapot Dome, Wyoming, were leased to private oil companies in exchange for bribes.

Photo courtesy of Franklin Roosevelt Library, NPx 65-590.

A side view of Eleanor's Val-Kill Cottage.

G. W. Harting photo courtesy of Franklin Roosevelt Library, NPx 72-168.1.

Nancy Cook in the Val-Kill
furniture shop in 1934.

Eleanor's Cottage

Franklin liked the female politicians who had become Eleanor's new friends. He particularly enjoyed talking to them about his favorite topic—politics. In the fall of 1924, he joined Eleanor, Nancy Cook, and Marion Dickerman for a picnic along the banks of Val-Kill Creek, near Sara's estate at Springwood. Looking at the sunlit fields, Eleanor lamented: "This is our last weekend because [Sara] is closing the house for the winter." Franklin turned to his wife and replied: "Why don't you build a cottage for yourselves?"

Why not indeed? The conversation snowballed into a full-fledged building project. Franklin soon sent a letter to a contractor:

> *My Missus and some of her female political friends want to build a shack on a stream in the back woods and want . . . to have the stream dug out so as to form an old-fashioned swimming hole.*

On January 1, 1926, the three women sat on barrels and ate their first meal at Val-Kill Cottage, a Dutch-style stone house. Nancy and Marion moved into the cottage immediately, and Eleanor joined them on weekends and holidays and during the summers. The three friends agreed that Nancy, a talented cabinetmaker, should build furniture for the cottage.

Nancy made such beautiful pieces that the women decided to open a small factory near the cottage. Nancy hired and supervised local craftsmen who made copies of Early American furniture. Franklin was one of the first customers of Val-Kill Industries, as the factory was known. He needed furniture to take to Warm Springs, Georgia, where he was spending more and more time.

Separate Lives

Franklin had visited Warm Springs, a run-down summer resort in southern Georgia, for the first time in 1924. When he got into the pool of natural mineral waters, he felt a surge of warmth flow over his crippled legs. By the end of his stay, he could walk in four feet of water without braces or crutches. "Warm Springs," said Franklin, "does my legs more good than anything else." In 1926, he loaned the Warm Springs Foundation a large sum of money to help them turn it into a treatment center for polio victims. Warm Springs became another home for Franklin; it was often referred to as the Little White House.

Eleanor never liked Warm Springs. She was depressed by the poverty and injustice of the segregated rural South. She preferred to stay in New York while Franklin's secretary, Marguerite ("Missy") LeHand, took care of activities at Warm Springs. As Franklin spent more time in Georgia, Eleanor spent more time parenting their five children.

Eleanor directed the children's education and suffered through their rebellious teenage years. Marion Dickerman and Nancy Cook often joined her as she took the children on picnics or camping trips. Eleanor knew it was important to spend this kind of time with her children, especially since Franklin could not.

Eleanor on the dock at Campobello with her sons John and Franklin Jr. in 1925.

Segregated:
Separated because of race, class, or ethnic origin.

The Little White House at Warm Springs, Georgia.

Ellis Island

Between 1892 and 1954,
poor immigrants entering the country
through the New York City harbor
had to undergo several hours of
medical and legal exams at the
Ellis Island Immigration Station.

In the picture above
a family of immigrants is waiting
at Ellis Island for entry into
the United States.

Photo courtesy of Library of Congress, LC B201 5202 14.

In 1926, Eleanor got a new chance to practice her child-rearing ideas. Marion Dickerman asked her to help buy the Todhunter School for Girls, where Marion worked as a teacher and vice principal. Eleanor jumped at the chance to follow in the footsteps of Mlle. Souvestre. The next year, she headed for New York City to work as a teacher.

Lively Lessons

Todhunter was a private school for girls aged 6 to 18. Eleanor taught courses in literature, drama, and history. She set high standards for her students and encouraged them to think independently. "Education only ends with death," Eleanor told them.

For lessons on modern history and current events, Eleanor used real-life examples. She preferred newspapers and magazines to textbooks. She took her students on field trips to City Hall, the courtrooms, Ellis Island, and the headquarters of the Democratic State Committee. Sometimes, she even took them into the slums. Later she wrote:

> *To these children of the rich, I had to explain what it meant . . .*
> *for a woman with her husband and eight children to live in*
> *three rooms in the basement.*

Eleanor's methods made the classroom come alive. "I never forgot a . . . thing she ever taught me," said one of her students. Eleanor, in turn, loved teaching. As Marion recalled, "Teaching gave her some of the happiest moments in her life."

Campaigning Again

It was no surprise that Eleanor had mixed feelings when the Democrats chose Franklin as their 1928 candidate for governor of New York, to replace Al Smith, their candidate for president. At first, Franklin resisted his party's nomination. He did not want to run for another public office until he could walk again. When Democratic leaders refused to take no for an answer, Franklin stopped returning their insistent phone calls. On the night of October 1, Al Smith asked Eleanor for help. She got Franklin on the line with Al Smith and left the room. As Eleanor later recalled: "I did not know until the following morning when I bought a newspaper that my husband had been persuaded . . . to accept the nomination."

As Eleanor had expected, the election brought Franklin new life. "If I could campaign another six months," he exclaimed, "I believe I could throw away my cane!" Franklin urged Eleanor to work for Al Smith's presidential campaign while he campaigned on his own. "I think he did not expect to carry the state if [Al] Smith lost the presidency," said Eleanor. Franklin was wrong. Although the Republicans defeated Al Smith by a landslide, Franklin carried New York by a paper-thin margin. He called himself the "one-half of one percent Governor."

Franklin Roosevelt with George Lunn, John Davis, and Al Smith in 1924.

The governor's mansion, Albany, New York.

Frank S. Landolfa photo courtesy of Franklin Roosevelt Library, NPx 69-11.

Eleanor watching craftsman
Frank Landolfa making furniture at
the Val-Kill furniture shop in 1931.

Photo courtesy of Franklin Roosevelt Library, NPx 48-22:3832(5), and CORBIS/Bettmann.

Eleanor was teaching at Todhunter
School around the time this portrait
was taken in August 1928.

Franklin's Eyes and Ears

Eleanor confided to a reporter that she was more upset by Al Smith's
defeat than she was pleased by Franklin's victory:

> *If the rest of the ticket didn't get in, what does it matter?*
> *No, I am not excited about my husband's election. I don't care.*
> *What difference can it make to me?*

The election results made a huge difference in Eleanor's life. "I know
if I take part in politics everyone will attribute anything I say or do to
Franklin," she explained. To avoid this, she resigned from her official
posts in the Democratic Party, but she did not give up all of her activities.

She would not quit her teaching job at Todhunter School. Nor would
she give up her co-ownership of the furniture factory at Val-Kill. She
continued to work behind the scenes at the state Democratic Party and
to support the League of Women Voters and the Women's Trade Union
League. Eleanor was changing the role of the political wife. A *New York
Times* headline announced:

> *Mrs. Roosevelt to Keep on Filling Many Jobs*
> *Besides Being the "First Lady" at Albany.*

Lorena Hickok, a reporter assigned to cover Franklin, was amazed at
Eleanor's energy and sense of adventure. Eleanor jumped at any chance
to try something new—a flight in a single-engine plane or a quick run
down an icy hill on an Olympic bobsled.

Lorena also got a firsthand look at the political partnership that was developing between Franklin and Eleanor. Because polio restricted Franklin's movements, he asked Eleanor to be his "eyes and ears." Each summer of his term, the couple checked on conditions in state institutions. Recalling the trips, Lorena wrote:

> *No public institution in the world ever got a more thorough going-over than Mrs. Roosevelt learned to give. . . . She would pull the covers off beds, examine the mattresses, look into dark corners, open closet doors. . . .*

Lorena Hickok.

A Winning Team

Most people considered Franklin a sure winner in the 1930 election for New York governor, but his reelection victory exceeded all forecasts. He even carried upstate New York—the first Democrat ever to do so.

Part of Franklin's success came from his swift action following the stock market crash of October 1929. In a matter of months, the United States economy went from "boom to bust," setting off a period known as the Great Depression. Millions of people lost their jobs. Businesses failed, banks closed, and factories shut down. Franklin won national attention by using state funds to give immediate relief to the unemployed and needy.

Great Depression:
A major slump in the U.S. economy, triggered in 1929 by a crash of the stock market.

A soup kitchen serving unemployed men during the Great Depression.

Bread lines:

During the Great Depression, unemployed people waited for hours in long lines to receive food.

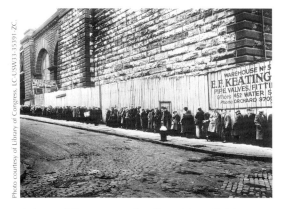

Photo courtesy of Library of Congress, LC-USW33-35391-ZC.

A bread line near the Brooklyn Bridge in New York City during the Great Depression.

Deadlocked:

A standstill that halts all progress on an action or decision.

Franklin had another reason for his success. Eleanor had touched people's hearts. She talked with voters face to face. With the help of her hardworking secretary Malvina ("Tommy") Thompson, she answered their letters. When the Depression hit, it was Eleanor, rather than Franklin, who visited the bread lines and spoke to people in the streets. She found it nearly impossible to turn away a hungry person.

The political team of Eleanor and Franklin did not escape the attention of Democratic officials who believed the pair could lead the party to the White House. Franklin was full of excitement when delegates placed his name on the ballot at the Democratic National Convention in June 1932. He sat next to the radio as the convention deadlocked over three candidates: Franklin Roosevelt, Al Smith, and Jack Garner, the popular Speaker of the House.

Eleanor dreaded the thought of Franklin's nomination for president. She confessed to Lorena Hickok, "I never wanted to be a President's wife, and I don't want it now."

No Ordinary

First Lady

Chapter 8   1932 - 1936

Key Events in Eleanor Roosevelt's Life

Key Events Around the World

1930

1932

When Franklin is elected president, Eleanor breaks the rules for first ladies by holding press conferences for women reporters only.

1933

1934

Adolf Hitler becomes the chancellor of Germany. The first concentration camp opens at Dachau. The "Bonus Army" returns to Washington, D.C.

Eleanor starts her syndicated column, "My Day."

1935

1936

Eleanor helps start the National Youth Administration (NYA) and helps women find jobs through the Works Progress Administration (WPA).

Poor farming techniques and several years of drought create a dust bowl in the prairie states, and dust storms affect the weather as far away as the eastern seaboard.

Eleanor tours and inspects federal work projects, reporting her findings to Franklin.

Congress passes the Social Security Act to provide benefits for the unemployed and the elderly. The National Labor Relations Act legalizes the right to collective bargaining.

1940

U.S. track star Jesse Owens wins four gold medals in the Olympic Games in Berlin, defying Hitler's theory of the superior Aryan race. *Life* magazine begins publication.

1945

1950

1955

As the deadlocked 1932 Democratic convention dragged on, Eleanor's uneasiness grew. Her future now rested in the hands of Franklin's two top political aides: Louis Howe, his adviser, and James Farley, the head of the New York State Democratic Committee. The two men worked around the clock to line up support for Franklin.

Eleanor's friends wondered what Eleanor would do if Franklin won the nomination. The answer came on the night of July 1, 1932. In a crowded room at the governor's mansion in Albany, a late-breaking radio report declared an end to the deadlock. California had switched its 44 votes from Jack Garner to Franklin Roosevelt. Grace Tully, one of Franklin's assistants, described the scene:

> *Mrs. Roosevelt and Missy LeHand embraced each other.*
> *Both embraced me. John and Elliott [Roosevelt] tossed scratch*
> *paper in the air and shook hands as if they hadn't seen each*
> *other in years. Mrs. Roosevelt came down out of the clouds*
> *before the rest of us. "I'm going to make some bacon and eggs,"*
> *she announced.*

Eleanor threw her support behind Franklin but vowed to Lorena Hickok that if he were elected, there would be no "First Lady of the Land." There would be only "plain, ordinary Mrs. Roosevelt." Describing her future, she declared: "I'll just have to go on being myself."

An aerial view of Chicago, Illinois, the site of the Democratic National Convention in 1932.

Eleanor swimming with Franklin's secretary, Missy LeHand.

Precedents:

Actions and decisions that serve as examples or models for future decisions.

New Deal:

Government-backed work programs established by President Franklin Roosevelt in the 1930s to create jobs for the unemployed during the Great Depression.

Molly Dewson, head of the women's division of the Democratic National Committee, with Eleanor and James Farley.

Breaking Rules

From the start, both Eleanor and Franklin set precedents. On July 2, the couple flew to Chicago to allow Franklin to accept the nomination in person. Never before had a presidential candidate and his wife taken a campaign trip by airplane. Franklin used the flight to prove that he looked to the future, not to the past. In his acceptance speech, he promised the country a New Deal.

Eleanor worked hard behind the scenes in Franklin's campaign. Working with a tough-minded, no-nonsense politician named Molly Dewson, she helped to mobilize the women's division of the Democratic National Committee. Eleanor and Molly printed millions of Rainbow Fliers—brightly colored leaflets that introduced Franklin and his New Deal to women voters.

Louis Howe gave Eleanor and Molly a list of "fighting states"—key states in which the election could be won or lost. In each of these states, Molly organized groups of "grass tramplers"—women who went from door to door to turn out the vote. They were so successful that Louis Howe declared he "would rather have a half-dozen women field workers than a hundred men any day."

Lorena Hickok, now covering both Eleanor and Franklin, admired the teamwork of the campaigning couple. Eleanor would walk where Franklin could not and tell him what she had seen. Lorena described the ordeal of trying to keep up with Eleanor:

I recall puffing, panting and perspiring as I followed her through a cornfield somewhere in Nebraska or Iowa. She moved swiftly, coolly and as easily as though she were accustomed to striding through a cornfield every day. . . .

The Listening Post

Eleanor set a busy pace for election day—November 8, 1932. She spent the morning teaching classes at the Todhunter School, then drove to Hyde Park to cast her ballot. Finally she and Franklin headed back to New York City to wait for election returns at the Biltmore Hotel. When the news came, it announced a stunning upset: Franklin had defeated his Republican rival, President Herbert Hoover, by a landslide.

News of Franklin's victory sent reporters scurrying to Eleanor's side. Although Eleanor kept smiling as she answered their questions, Lorena noticed a deep sadness in her eyes. Lorena wrote: "I was reminded of a fox, surrounded by a pack of . . . hounds." In the days following the election, Eleanor pleaded for a few more months of freedom.

I shall drop a good many things when we get to Washington. But . . . we aren't in Washington yet. . . . Until March 4, [1933,] I hope to be permitted to enjoy the privileges accorded a private citizen.

Her request made life difficult for the Secret Service agents who showed up at the Roosevelt townhouse on East 65th Street. Although Franklin accepted their presence, Eleanor waved them away. "Nobody is going to hurt me," she declared. "I'm not important enough."

Eleanor casting her vote in Hyde Park.

Eleanor riding horses with Mrs. Henry Morgenthau in Rock Creek Park, Washington, D.C., March 1933.

Photo courtesy of Library of Congress, LC-USZ62-108091.

Eleanor Roosevelt in 1933.

When Eleanor returned to teaching on November 9, she made no mention of the election. Her students, however, beamed with pride. "We think it's grand to have the wife of the President for our teacher," one girl exclaimed. "I don't want you to think of me that way," replied Eleanor with a smile. "I'm just the same as I was yesterday."

But nothing was to stay the same for Eleanor. Franklin soon asked her to give up her teaching position and to stop her committee work. He felt she should focus on her new role as first lady. Leaving her teaching job was Eleanor's most painful loss. In an interview with Lorena, she said: "I wonder if you have any idea how I hate to [quit]. I've liked [teaching] more than anything else I've ever done."

Eleanor gave up her jobs, but she did not give up her desire to help other people. At a farewell dinner given in Eleanor's honor by friends at the Women's Trade Union League, she declared:

> *I truly believe that I understand what faces the great masses*
> *of people in the country today. I have no illusions that anyone*
> *can change the world in a short time. . . . Yet I do believe*
> *that even a few people, who want . . . to do the right thing . . .*
> *can help.*

Armed with this belief, Eleanor pledged that she would serve as a "listening post" for Franklin and continue to be his "eyes and ears."

Eleanor as Agitator

Just before Franklin's inauguration, Eleanor went to Washington, D.C., to make plans for their move to the White House. Instead of Secret Service agents, she took Louis Howe, Lorena Hickok, and her son Elliott. She traveled by public train and refused the help of White House aides or a limousine. When a State Department official tried to drive her to the White House, Eleanor said she would walk. "You can't do that!" protested the official. "Oh, yes, I can," replied Eleanor.

With Lorena at her side, she set out on foot, breaking the first of many White House rules. Along the way, an elderly woman called out: "Good luck, Mrs. Roosevelt!"

Eleanor welcomed all the luck she could get. By early 1933, she knew that the country faced one of the most serious crises in its history. More than 85,000 businesses had failed since 1929. The national income of the United States had dropped by nearly 50 percent. More than 13 million people—25 percent of the work force—were unemployed. Hungry, homeless people depended on soup kitchens or garbage cans for their next meal. On the night of Franklin's inauguration, Eleanor asked: "How much can people take without blowing up?"

Franklin took Eleanor's question seriously. He believed government needed to move quickly to restore people's faith in their leaders and in themselves. On March 4, 1933, Franklin delivered the first radio broadcast of an inaugural address. As millions of people listened, he declared: "This nation asks for action, and action now."

The first lady arriving at the Inaugural Ball in 1933.

Eleanor serving food in a soup kitchen in 1932.

Franklin compared the Depression to war and pledged himself to victory. He promised to ask Congress to give him power equal to "the power that would be given to me if we were in fact invaded by a foreign foe." In words ringing with hope, he told Americans: "The only thing we have to fear is fear itself."

On March 6, two days after the inauguration, Eleanor held a press conference. With the support of Franklin and Louis Howe, she invited 35 women reporters. The meeting was another first. No first lady had ever held a press conference, and never had one been held for women only! Over the next 12 years, Eleanor would hold 348 "women-only" press conferences. Once when the king of England tried to sneak in, Eleanor politely asked him to leave.

Eleanor defended her "women-only" policy as a way of guaranteeing jobs to women reporters, who were rare. The policy also allowed her to discuss topics of special interest to women. Male reporters protested—especially when Eleanor gave the women leads on political news.

Franklin used Eleanor's press conferences as a sounding board for policies he did not want to discuss himself. As Eleanor explained: "I'm the agitator; he's the politician." Whenever she said something that caused a stir, Franklin threw up his hands and said: "That's my wife, and I can't be expected to do anything about her."

Harris Ewing photo courtesy of Franklin Roosevelt Library, NPx 8-22:372(4)6).

Only women reporters were invited to the first lady's press conferences.

Franklin's Secret Weapon

The staff that ran the White House threw up their hands, too. Eleanor ran the elevators herself. She moved her own furniture. She changed beds and swept floors. Watching the shocked faces of the White House staff, Eleanor's cousin Alice joked: "Out with the old, in with the radical!"

In a time of economic hardship, Eleanor felt she and the rest of the White House should set an example by being thrifty. She wore simple $10 dresses. With thousands of people hungry, she served "square meals" that cost pennies a serving. At a "7-cent luncheon," she served guests hot stuffed eggs with tomato sauce, mashed potatoes, bread, prune pudding, and coffee. Instead of using the White House limousine, she bought a light blue roadster and announced that she would drive it herself without a police escort. Her friends knew it would not be long before she headed out on one of her famous inspection trips.

In late March 1933, an 81-year-old social reformer named Charlotte Everett Hopkins asked Eleanor to tour the slums of the nation's capital. Eleanor drove her car through the poor neighborhoods and back alleys of Washington. She reported her findings to the press—and to Franklin—promising that the president would soon back a housing bill to clean up the slums.

In July 1933, Eleanor took the roadster on another trip. Louis Howe wanted Eleanor to visit the camp of the Bonus Army in a park near Washington, D.C. When the Bonus Army had marched on Washington, D.C., in 1932, President Herbert Hoover called out armed troops to turn them away. This time, Franklin made sure the veterans were offered

Thrifty:

To be practical with money; a wise investor.

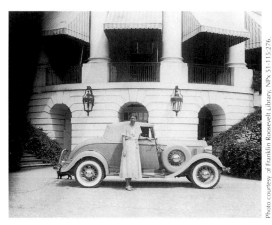

Photo courtesy of Franklin Roosevelt Library, NPx 51-115-276.

Eleanor with her new roadster in front of the South Portico of the White House in 1933.

Roadster:

An open-air automobile with a single seat in the front and a rumble seat, or pull-down seat, in the back.

Bonus Army:

The Bonus Army was made up of thousands of jobless World War I veterans and their families, demanding payment of a pension bonus promised to them after the war.

A. S. Foster drawing courtesy of the Franklin Roosevelt Library, NPx 55-623.

"Going or coming, I wonder?"

An A. S. Foster cartoon of the Roosevelts' dog, Fala, asking: "Going or coming, I wonder?"

Photo courtesy of CORBIS-Bettmann, U221915ACME>1.

Eleanor with Amelia Earhart, promoting passenger air travel on a flight from Baltimore, Maryland, to Washington, D.C., in 1933.

housing, food, medical services, and jobs. When the marchers still refused to go home, Louis used Franklin's secret weapon—Eleanor.

While Louis sat in the car, Eleanor toured the camp alone. She walked through rows of tents and stopped to talk to marchers waiting in line for food. The surprised marchers asked the first lady to make a short speech, so she shared her memories of World War I, telling them: "I shall always be grateful to those who served their country."

The marchers cheered Eleanor when she turned to walk back to her car. Recalling the scene, one marcher wrote: "Hoover sent the army. Roosevelt sent his wife." The marchers soon voted to go home.

Eleanor Everywhere

Eleanor's visit with the Bonus Army convinced people that the government cared about their suffering. In the first 100 days of his administration, Franklin pushed through legislation to put his New Deal into place. To drum up support for the New Deal, Franklin encouraged Eleanor to make other appearances.

In the 12 months following Franklin's inauguration, Eleanor covered more than 40,000 miles by car, train, and plane. She enjoyed flying so much that she invited the pioneering woman pilot Amelia Earhart to the White House for dinner. Amelia asked Eleanor to join her for an evening flight over the capital to promote passenger air travel. Wearing long evening gowns, the two women took a short flight from Washington, D.C., to Baltimore, Maryland. A reporter later asked Eleanor how she felt about flying with a woman. Her reply: "I'd give a lot to do it myself!"

The nation had never seen a first lady like Eleanor Roosevelt. She turned up in so many places that the press nicknamed her Eleanor Everywhere. Her comings and goings made headline news. She visited coal miners in West Virginia and talked with migrant workers in California. She toured the slums of Puerto Rico and sat with sharecroppers in their tarpaper shacks in the South. Wherever she went, Eleanor treated people with respect. She listened to their problems and then promptly asked: "What can I do for you?"

Eleanor carried her findings back to Franklin. He began many meetings with the words "You know my Missus gets around a lot." His advisers soon learned that these words signaled the start of a new program. Although Eleanor denied that she helped Franklin make decisions, most observers believed otherwise. As one of Franklin's advisers wrote:

> *No one who ever saw Eleanor Roosevelt sit down facing her*
> *husband, and, holding his eye firmly, say to him, "Franklin,*
> *I think you should . . ." or, "Franklin, surely you will not . . ."*
> *will ever forget the experience.*

A Woman of Words

Eleanor worked tirelessly to defend the programs she supported. She continued to write the newspaper and magazine articles she had started in the 1920s. In 1933, she agreed to write a monthly column for the *Woman's Home Companion*. In the next six months, more than 300,000

Migrant workers:
Workers who move from one harvest to another,
following the growing season from south to
north, to remain employed full time.

Sharecroppers:
Farmers who give a share of their crops to
landlords in exchange for the use of the land,
housing, tools, and seeds.

Eleanor puts on a miner's helmet and rides with the miners down into an Ohio coal mine in 1935.

Photo courtesy of Franklin Roosevelt Library, NPx 64-335.

Drawing courtesy of Franklin Roosevelt Library, NPx 73-13.

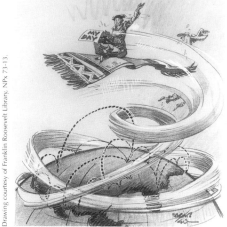

A 1940 political cartoon of Eleanor traveling the globe on a flying carpet while writing her column, "My Day."

Top: Eleanor visits Puerto Rico and the Virgin Islands with James Bourne and Lorena Hickok in 1934.

letters poured in to the White House. Eleanor made sure each letter was answered, either by herself or by the appropriate government agency.

Two years later, Eleanor started a column in the *Ladies' Home Journal* called "My Day." For the rest of her life, she would write this column six days a week, no matter where she was—on an airplane, on a battleship, or on her sickbed. She took credit—or blame—for every word she wrote. By the end of 1936, the column ran in 62 papers, reaching more than four million readers.

Eleanor also toured the country to give lectures. When people criticized her for accepting money for lectures and articles, Eleanor defended herself as a working woman paid fairly for her skills. She pointed out that she gave much of her income to charities and paid for most of her own expenses.

Clearly, Eleanor Roosevelt had become a political force on her own. Rival columnist Westbrook Pegler wrote:

> *I think we can take the wraps off and call her the greatest American woman, because there is no other who works as hard or knows the low-down truth about the people and the troubles in their hearts as well as she does.*

As the 1936 presidential election approached, Republicans realized that they had to plan a strategy against both Franklin *and* Eleanor. The first lady who had broken all the rules should make a good target.

A *Voice* for the ·P·e·o·p·l·e

Chapter 9

1936 - 1941

Key Events in Eleanor Roosevelt's Life

Eleanor meets with Mary McLeod Bethune and recommends her for a position at the NYA. Eleanor and Franklin mourn the death of Louis Howe.

Eleanor visits the Highlander Folk School and attends the Southern Conference for Human Welfare.

Eleanor addresses the Democratic National Convention, asking for support for Franklin's choice of a vice presidential candidate for his third term.

1935
1936
1937
1938
1939
1940
1941

1945

1950

1955

1960

Key Events Around the World

Amelia Earhart's plane disappears somewhere in the South Pacific while she attempts an around-the-world solo flight.

The Fair Labor Standards Act limits the number of hours that can be worked without overtime (44) and sets a minimum wage (25 cents an hour). Action Comics introduces *Superman*.

African-American opera singer Marian Anderson performs at the Lincoln Memorial after being refused the use of Constitution Hall.

Dr. Charles Drew develops a way to store blood, leading to the beginning of blood banks. Winston Churchill becomes the prime minister of Great Britain, as Germany threatens to strike by air.

Adolf Hitler gives orders to begin the extermination of more than six million Jews. The Japanese bomb Pearl Harbor, Hawaii, causing the United States to enter WWII.

Late in 1935, Louis Howe walked into the first lady's office and said: "Eleanor, if you want to be President in 1940, tell me now so I can start getting things ready." Louis believed Franklin would be reelected in 1936. But what about 1940? No president had ever sought three terms of office. Louis thought Eleanor would be the ideal candidate to run in his place.

A startled Eleanor turned down Louis's offer. "I do not think we have yet reached the point where the majority of our people would . . . follow the leadership . . . of a woman as President," she explained.

Louis had little time to change Eleanor's mind. Years of smoking cigarettes had taken their toll on his lungs. On April 18, 1936, Louis died while plotting Franklin's reelection campaign. Keenly feeling the loss, Eleanor and Franklin—the political team that Louis had helped build—were now on their own.

Eleanor and Franklin had to campaign for the 1936 election without the help of Louis Howe.

Roosevelts in Demand

Eleanor tried to keep a low profile at the Democratic National Convention in June. Women at the convention, however, took great pride in Eleanor's accomplishments as first lady. Secretary of Labor Frances Perkins—the first woman to hold a cabinet post—brought women delegates to their feet when she declared: "I know that many women in this country when they go to vote in November for Franklin Roosevelt will be thinking . . . of Eleanor Roosevelt."

Frances Perkins.

Cabinet:
A body of presidential appointees who advise the president and head up the major departments within the government.

Photo courtesy of CORBIS/Bettmann, VV6772.

Mrs. Roosevelt at the President's Birthday Ball in January 1936, shortly after the inauguration for Franklin's second term.

Eleanor remained a reluctant first lady. When Franklin won the Democratic nomination overwhelmingly, she wrote:

> *For the good of the country[,] . . . it is . . . to be hoped that he will be reelected, but from a personal point of view I am quite overcome when I think of four years more of the life I have been leading!*

The Republicans made an issue of Eleanor's busy life. They nominated Kansas governor Alf Landon as their candidate, and Landon's wife made it clear that she would not join her husband on the campaign trail. "Mrs. Alf M. Landon . . . will devote the time from now until the election to the care of her family," declared one newspaper story. Nor would she follow in Eleanor's footsteps if Alf was elected. "Mrs. Landon will spend her time in the White House," promised Republican speakers.

Although Democratic advisers suggested that Eleanor stay in the background, voters had other ideas. As reporter Ruth Finnley explained:

> *The crowds wanted Mrs. Roosevelt. If she failed to appear on the platform they shouted for her until she did appear, and they cheered her just as heartily as her husband, sometimes more heartily.*

In the end, Franklin defeated Landon by more than 11 million votes. Eleanor found the results "a little awe-inspiring." She told Franklin: "You could be a king or a dictator and they'd fight for you! Lucky you have no such aspirations!"

Eleanor had reason to fear the abuse of power by a dictator. By 1936, dictators had grabbed power in several nations around the world—Spain, Italy, Germany, Russia, and Japan. The Depression was worldwide, and these leaders justified their iron-fisted rule by blaming their economic woes on other ethnic groups or nations.

Eleanor believed that government belonged to the many, not to the few. Even in America, however, not everyone could participate in the government. Eleanor made it her business to listen to these forgotten groups—and to make sure that Franklin listened, too. Three groups attracted her special attention: women, African Americans, and youth.

Dictator:

A ruler who has absolute authority over the government of a country. Such a government would be called a dictatorship.

Opening Doors

Eleanor remembered the time when male delegates shut women out of platform meetings at the 1924 Democratic convention. As first lady, Eleanor wanted no closed doors at the White House—especially for women.

When Eleanor invited women leaders to present their ideas at her weekly press conferences, she sent their suggestions to government officials, along with a note that read: "Will you look into this? E.R."

Women sewing in a factory in 1936.

Lewis Hine photo courtesy of National Archives, 136.69-RP-56, American Image Collection.

Photo courtesy of Library of Congress, LC-USZ62-98833.

Labor leader Mary Anderson, head of the women's bureau of the Department of Labor, in 1942. Behind her is a painting of women factory workers.

She gave women access to the president. As Molly Dewson, the head of the Women's Division of the Democratic National Committee, explained:

> *When I wanted help on some definite point, Mrs. Roosevelt gave me the opportunity to sit by the President at dinner and the matter was settled before we finished our soup.*

During the New Deal, women held a record number of government posts. Eleanor regularly reviewed the lists of appointments for government positions. If there were no women on the list, Franklin heard about it. As Eleanor later admitted:

> *I might go to my husband and say that I was very weary of reminding him . . . that women were in existence. . . . He always smiled and said: "Of course; I thought a woman's name had been put on the list."*

Franklin would then tell Eleanor: "Have someone call up and say I feel a woman should be recognized." Eleanor would place the call herself and suggest a few names. The names that she mentioned often came from Molly Dewson, who had backed the appointment of Frances Perkins as Secretary of Labor. Together, Eleanor and Molly made sure that women were represented at nearly every level of the Roosevelt administration.

Women demanded and won a new role in the Democratic Party. In 1936, women delegates helped draft the party platform—a measure of how far they had come since 1924.

The Human Face of Suffering

The 1936 Democratic platform supported and expanded the New Deal. At the heart of the New Deal were government-backed work programs that created jobs for the unemployed. Eleanor visited a number of these programs and learned that many jobs were reserved for men only. Yet nearly two million women were unemployed during the Depression. Prodded by Eleanor, the 1935 Works Progress Administration (WPA) eventually employed between 300,000 and 400,000 women a year.

Eleanor had to fight to keep these programs alive. When the Depression continued into Franklin's second term, some critics of the New Deal accused Franklin of creating a budget deficit by wasting tax dollars on the needy. Eleanor defended unemployment programs by putting a human face on the suffering. She told the stories of real people in her "My Day" column.

> A woman writes me: "I have a family of six. Our WPA pay has been $42.50 a month. We haven't saved anything on that, could you? . . . How do we live, Mrs. Roosevelt . . . ?"

Other critics charged that government programs promoted Communism. In 1938, Eleanor told reporters: "We need not fear any 'isms' if our democracy is achieving the ends for which it was established." In Eleanor's mind, these ends included economic security and justice for all.

Works Progress Administration (WPA):
Part of the New Deal, the WPA employed many people to work on government construction projects, putting them back to work during the Great Depression.

Budget deficit:
A budget deficit occurs when spending exceeds the revenue that is available.

Photo courtesy of Franklin Roosevelt Library, NPx 63-424.

A work crew hired through the Works Progress Administration (WPA) clears debris from a flooded street in Kentucky.

Photo courtesy of Library of Congress, LC-US262-115416.

Discrimination:

Unfair or unequal behavior toward a group or an individual because of race, gender, class, disability, or national origin.

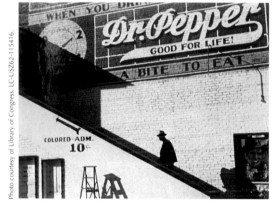

A segregated movie theater in 1939.

Lynchings:

Unlawful execution by hanging without a trial by jury, usually racially motivated.

She explained that "government has a responsibility to defend the weak." Eleanor used her position as first lady to call attention to one of the biggest injustices of the 1930s—discrimination against African Americans.

Taking a Stand

Racial discrimination was widespread in the United States. African Americans were segregated into separate housing, schools, restaurants, churches, and seats on public transportation. In much of the nation, African Americans worked at the least desirable jobs for the lowest pay. Even in the best of times, they were often the last hired and the first fired.

When the Depression hit, black Americans had a far higher unemployment rate than white Americans. They placed their hopes in the New Deal, yet discrimination kept them from getting a fair share of its benefits. When Eleanor made Franklin aware of this situation, he delayed taking action. To get his programs through Congress, he needed the votes of white politicians. As Franklin told Eleanor: "I can't . . . [lose] certain votes . . . by pushing any measure that would entail a fight."

But Eleanor would not back down. She had seen African-American children denied an equal education. She had read about lynchings in the South. She had met with the leaders of the civil-rights movement. These experiences led Eleanor to join African Americans in their fight for justice.

Eleanor's views on civil rights became well known. Newspapers carried photographs of her with African-American miners, sharecroppers, and schoolchildren. She led cabinet and congressional wives on walking tours of poor, segregated neighborhoods. She joined the National Association for the Advancement of Colored People (NAACP) and the National Urban League—two groups leading the civil-rights movement. She attacked racial discrimination in radio addresses:

We can have no group beaten down. . . . We must learn to work together, all of us, regardless of race, creed or color. We must wipe out the feeling of intolerance wherever we find it.

As Eleanor had done for women, she pressured Franklin to bring African Americans into government. She championed a group known as the "Black Cabinet," African-American leaders who became informal advisers to the president. Members included educator Mary McLeod Bethune and lawyer Robert C. Weaver.

Eleanor's stand on civil rights helped bring about a major change in voting patterns. In the past, African Americans had voted for the Republicans—the party of Abraham Lincoln. During the New Deal, they switched in record numbers to the Democratic Party. They did this, said NAACP leader Roy Wilkins, because of Eleanor's "personal fight against discrimination."

Civil rights:
Basic rights granted to all citizens of the United States, such as the right to vote.

National Association for the Advancement of Colored People (NAACP):
Created in 1909, the NAACP protects the rights and welfare of all people of color.

Photo courtesy of Library of Congress, LC-USW3-13518.

Mary McLeod Bethune.

Photo courtesy of Library of Congress, LC-USZ62-109644.

Photo courtesy of AP/Wide World Photos.

In November 1938, Eleanor addressed the Southern Conference for Human Welfare in Birmingham, Alabama.

Top: Pauli Murray as a "young firebrand."

Backlash:
A strong, negative reaction to an action, situation, or idea.

Firebrands:
A nickname for people who boldly speak out about particular causes and issues.

"Riled Up"

In 1938, a young teacher for the WPA was denied admission to an all-white graduate school in North Carolina. Her rejection letter read: "Members of your race are not admitted to the University." In an angry letter to Eleanor, the teacher, Pauli Murray, asked: "What does this mean for Negro-Americans? . . . [D]oes it mean that everything you said has no meaning for us?"

Eleanor responded to Pauli's letter. She had just returned from a trip to Birmingham, Alabama, where she had seen segregation in action. Attending a meeting on economic conditions in the South, Eleanor noticed that blacks and whites were forced to sit in separate sections. Rather than accept this situation, she asked that her chair be placed between the two sections. During the meeting, Eleanor further upset southern lawmakers by challenging them to come up with a plan for ending racial violence—not just in the South, but in the whole nation.

Eleanor encouraged Pauli to write regularly. From Pauli, Eleanor learned about a new generation of African Americans who were impatient for change. Leaders included NAACP lawyer Thurgood Marshall and author Richard Wright. Eleanor admired them, but she feared a white backlash. She advised Pauli, "Don't push too fast." However, Eleanor did not always follow her own advice. As Pauli later told Eleanor:

> *One of the reasons we "firebrands" (your own term) love you so is that when you're "riled up," you're a bit of a firebrand yourself.*

Eleanor got "riled up" in 1939 when the Daughters of the American Revolution (DAR) banned African-American opera singer Marian Anderson from performing at Constitution Hall. Eleanor, a longtime member of the DAR, made headline news by resigning from the organization in protest. A poll showed that 67 percent of the American people supported Eleanor's decision.

With Eleanor's help, Marian Anderson gave a free open air concert at the Lincoln Memorial. More than 75,000 people were on hand to hear Marian sing. NAACP leader Walter White called the concert "one of the most thrilling experiences of our time."

Three months later, Eleanor presented Marian with the NAACP's Spingarn Medal, an award given annually for African-American achievement. A leading African-American newspaper described the scene as "a great occasion surpassed only by the greatness of Mrs. Roosevelt."

Saving a Generation

Another group that claimed Eleanor's heart was the nation's youth. By the mid-1930s, nearly five million people younger than age 25 were out of work. Millions more tried to get by on part-time wages. They could not afford to attend college or start families. In an interview, Eleanor declared:

> *I have moments of real terror when I think we may be losing this generation. We have got to bring these young people into the active life of the community and make them feel that they are necessary.*

Daughters of the American Revolution (DAR):
A patriotic society formed in 1890 for women whose ancestors fought in the American Revolution.

Marian Anderson singing at the Lincoln Memorial in Washington, D.C., in 1939.

An unemployed youth in Washington, D.C., during the Great Depression.

Photo courtesy of Library of Congress, LC-USZ62-36963.

National Youth Administration (NYA):

A New Deal program created in 1935 to help young people find part-time employment.

Vocational training:

Training for a particular job skill.

Newsreels:

Short films featuring news events from around the world; these were usually shown before a feature film at a movie theater.

Harry Hopkins.

Eleanor enlisted Harry Hopkins, the head of the WPA, in her battle to help the youth. In June 1935, they persuaded Franklin to create the National Youth Administration (NYA). The agency provided part-time jobs for 600,000 college students and vocational training for more than a million others. To make sure these benefits were distributed fairly, the NYA included an Office of Minority Affairs, which was headed by Mary McLeod Bethune.

Eleanor believed the NYA was one of her greatest accomplishments: "I was very proud that the right thing was done regardless of the political consequences." She used her "My Day" columns to gain support for the NYA and to respond to its many critics. As newsreels showed armies of youth saluting Adolf Hitler in Nazi Germany, some of Franklin's advisers warned that voters might think he was using government funds to control the minds of American youth. To put people's fears at rest, Eleanor visited at least 112 NYA sites and wrote about the benefits of its programs.

Defending Democracy

Like Eleanor, Franklin believed that democracy had taught American youth to be independent thinkers. In 1935, a group of young people proved him right by organizing the American Youth Congress (AYC). AYC members wanted the government to put billions of dollars into youth programs—even if it meant taking money from the national defense and industry. In 1936, they invited Eleanor to meet with them.

Franklin's advisers warned Eleanor that the AYC was too radical. Eleanor met with them anyway. Although they peppered her with questions, the heated exchange of ideas energized her. She understood the sources of youthful anger and learned why many of the AYC members were attracted to socialism. Eleanor had a chance to defend democracy and to suggest ways the AYC could bring about nonviolent social change.

Reporter Ruby Black wrote that Eleanor's activities with the AYC "brought more criticism upon her . . . than anything else she did." Eleanor's critics even accused her of promoting Communism.

The charges against Eleanor grew louder when people learned of her involvement with the Highlander Folk School in Tennessee. Founded in 1932 by Myles Horton, the Highlander School welcomed people of all races. The school taught students skilled trades and how to work together to bring about change. Supporting unions and civil rights, it taught students nonviolent protest methods such as sit-ins and strikes. Eleanor's support of the school convinced her critics they were right.

In November 1939, Eleanor surprised the Congress by showing up at the hearings of the House Un-American Activities Committee. The hearings had been organized to investigate groups suspected of Communist activities—including the AYC, the Highlander Folk School, and some officials of the New Deal. Eleanor told the investigators: "I just came to listen." She then sat down at the press table and took notes.

Radical:
Favoring extreme changes.

Socialism:
An economic system that places government controls on the production and distribution of goods and services.

Sit-ins:
Acts of nonviolent protest that encourage participants to sit down in a central area of business, government, or education and refuse to move until their demands are met.

Eleanor visiting with Myles Horton while attending the Southern Conference for Human Welfare in Chattanooga, Tennessee, in 1939.

Photo courtesy of National Archives, 306-PS-51-9773.

German soldiers on motorcycles ride through a bombed town in Poland in 1939.

Eleanor turned her notes into "My Day" columns. She asked whether everyone who disagreed with the government should be called a Communist. She also suggested that the hearings violated the right to free speech and trial by jury—rights granted by the Bill of Rights and the U.S. Constitution.

> *Let's fight for our Democracy and our Bill of Rights, and wherever we find things in which we do not believe, let's be free to express ourselves.*

Eleanor wrote these words at a time when she strongly opposed the AYC's support of Russia. In August 1939, Germany and Russia had signed a pact in which they agreed to divide up Poland but not to attack each other. Although Eleanor disagreed with the AYC, she continued to defend their right to speak freely.

Extraordinary Circumstances

By 1940, the constant criticisms and accusations had made Eleanor long to leave the White House, in spite of the voices of people who wanted her to stay. Journalist William Allen White echoed the suggestion Louis Howe had made in 1935: that Eleanor should run for president. He said, "Every time she does anything she reminds me of T.R."

Eleanor's response was blunt: "Nothing on [this] green earth would induce me to run for anything." She also refused to commit Franklin to a third term. Traditionally, no president had ever served more than two terms.

The extraordinary circumstances of 1940 called for a break in tradition. At home, the Depression continued to cause misery. Overseas, the German invasion of Poland had triggered the Second World War. The Axis powers—Germany, Italy, and Japan—invaded nation after nation. Franklin admitted that he was "a tired and weary man" and would run only if asked.

At the 1940 Democratic convention, Franklin's aides told the assembled delegates that he would not seek the nomination. After a stunned silence, the loudspeakers began to crackle: "We want Roosevelt!" The growing clamor gave Franklin the nomination, but the delegates were divided on a nominee for vice president. Franklin asked Eleanor to speak in favor of his choice, Henry Wallace.

Never before had a first lady addressed a national convention. Without any notes, Eleanor faced a crowd of more than 50,000 people:

> *This is no ordinary time. . . . No man who is a candidate for President or who is President can carry this situation alone. This is carried only by a united people who love their country.*

Eleanor's speech ended the debate. The delegates handed Franklin his choice of vice president. A short time later, Franklin delivered his acceptance speech from the White House, reminding delegates that it was now up to voters to break the two-term tradition.

Axis powers:

The Axis powers fought against the Allies in World War II. They included Germany, Italy, and Japan.

Eleanor addressing the Democratic National Convention in Chicago, Illinois, in 1940.

Photo courtesy of Franklin Roosevelt Library, NPx 6-1311(16), and CORBIS/Bettmann.

Photo from *Life* magazine courtesy of Associated Press.

Eleanor models her mother's tiger-claw necklace for actors Pat O'Brien and Jimmy Cagney at her 56th birthday celebration.

Unprecedented:
Something that has never happened before.

The Republicans waged a hard-fought campaign. Republican nominee Wendell Wilkie claimed that a third-term presidency would open the door to a dictatorship. He attacked the New Deal and the first lady, handing out buttons that read, "We Don't Want Eleanor Either."

On election day, a record 50 million voters went to the polls and elected Franklin to an unprecedented third term, by a margin of five million votes.

Eleanor, who was now 56 years old, received a letter from her good friend Lorena Hickok: "I'd never have believed it possible for a woman to develop after 50 as you have in the last six years." But Eleanor's transformation was not complete. She would expand her role as a radical first lady and move onto the world stage as well.

Photo courtesy of Library of Congress, LC-USZ62-116994.

A young polio victim admiring a poster of President Roosevelt.

First Lady

of the

·World

Chapter 10

1941 - 1945

Key Events in Eleanor Roosevelt's Life

Key Events Around the World

1940	
1941	
1942	
1943	
1944	
1945	

Eleanor visits defense plants and the Japanese internment camp at Gila River, Arizona.

Japanese Americans are confined in internment camps until the end of World War II.

Eleanor visits New Zealand and the South Pacific on behalf of the Red Cross.

Antibiotics are discovered in forms useful for treating infection in soldiers on the front lines.

Franklin and Eleanor prepare for a fourth term in the White House as the war rages on all fronts.

Congressman James William Fulbright introduces a bill to set up the United Nations.

In February, Franklin goes to Europe for a peace conference at Yalta. In April, he dies of a cerebral hemorrhage at Warm Springs, Georgia.

General Dwight Eisenhower orders the D-Day invasion of Normandy, France.

Fifty nations gather in San Francisco to draft the charter for the United Nations.

1950

1955

1960

1965

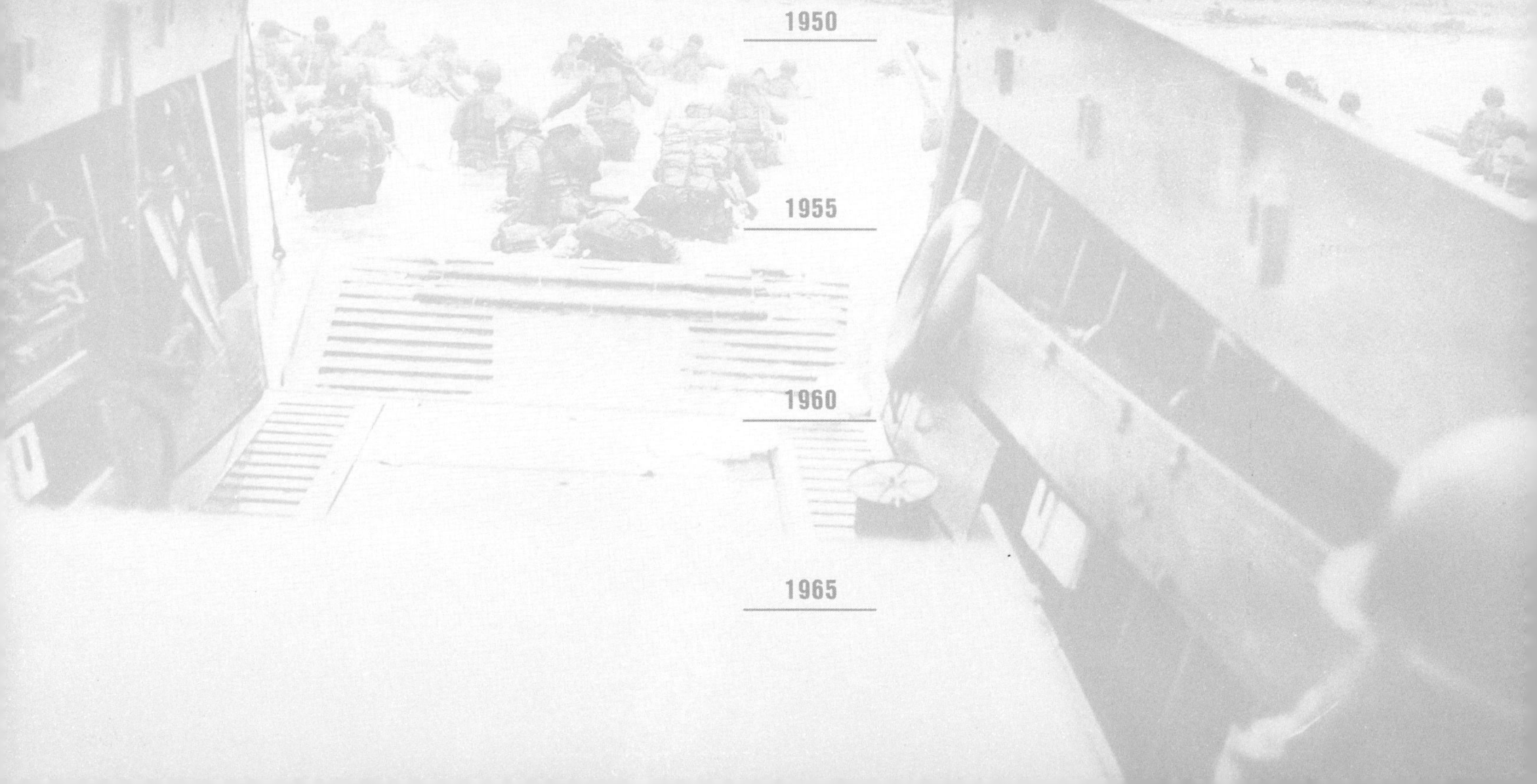

As German bombs rained down on Europe, Eleanor used her "My Day" columns to condemn the Axis powers for spreading totalitarianism around the world. She also openly praised Great Britain—the unconquered leader of the Allies—for defying the German bombs.

Eleanor tried to keep Americans informed about what was happening in Europe. The words and actions of Adolf Hitler, the German dictator, were especially alarming to Eleanor. The Nazi leader blamed the Jewish people for Germany's economic problems and called for their destruction.

Eleanor sympathized with the refugees who begged the United States to open its doors. Hoping to make it easier for German Jews to escape Hitler's reach, Eleanor supported a bill that would admit 10,000 children a year for two years, more than the usual number of immigrants allowed from Germany. The bill was attacked by isolationists who wanted to cut immigration. Eleanor reminded them that the United States was a nation of immigrants.

The Child Refugee Bill was eventually withdrawn, but Eleanor did not give up her fight. In 1941, as the Nazis herded Jews into concentration camps in Poland and Russia, she told the readers of "My Day":

> These mass removals, where people are treated like animals
> and not like human beings, are so horrible to contemplate that
> one can only hope that at a certain point feelings become
> numb. . . .

Photo courtesy of Library of Congress, LC-USZ62-61239.

German air raids over St. Patrick's Cathedral in London in 1940.

Totalitarianism:
Government control of all political, social, and economic activities of a nation.

Refugees:
People who flee to another country because of a hostile invasion or acts of persecution in their own country.

Immigration:
The arrival of people into a country, with the intent to live permanently in that country. The one who arrives is called an immigrant.

Concentration camps:
Camps set up by Nazi Germany to imprison and execute millions of Jewish people and their supporters.

Jewish people in Warsaw, Poland, during World War II, on their way to Nazi concentration camps.

Draft:

Mandatory service in the military; usually activated during times of war.

Eleanor attending a rally with labor leader A. Philip Randolph.

Eleanor's feelings never became numb. The sufferings of persecuted people during World War II motivated her campaign to protect the rights of human beings everywhere.

Threats to Democracy

Threats to democracy overseas made Eleanor more aware of threats to democracy at home. Franklin knew the United States would have to help the Allies win the war in Europe. When he began preparing the nation for this effort, Eleanor supported him.

Americans still suffering from the effects of the Great Depression protested the president's idea of converting peacetime factories to war industries. They thought that government money should be spent on helping people at home instead of making guns for a war in Europe.

Eleanor saw the lack of equal rights for African Americans as another threat to democracy. When Franklin called for a peacetime draft, African-American leaders asked for a cabinet-level meeting to end discrimination in the military. Eleanor was in favor of the meeting. She knew that African Americans could only serve in segregated army units and that they were barred entirely from the Army Air Corps and the Marines. In the navy, they worked mostly as cooks or janitors. When Franklin stalled, Eleanor pushed him to move forward with the meeting.

NAACP leader Walter White later sent Eleanor a note thanking her for intervening with the president. As a result of the meeting, African Americans entered all branches of the military service. Some of them won distinction as high-level officers, including Benjamin O. Davis—the army's first African-American general. Despite these victories, African Americans did not gain the right they most wanted—integrated military units. Eleanor wrote in 1942: "[Negroes] are drafted into the Army and expected to fight for a country which denies them the rights guaranteed to every citizen in our Constitution."

Eleanor also backed African-American demands for a fair share of jobs in the defense industries. To make sure the demands of African Americans were heard, labor and civil-rights leader A. Philip Randolph organized a march on Washington, D.C., in May 1941. Franklin asked Eleanor to talk Randolph out of the march. Eleanor failed to do this but urged Franklin to meet with Randolph privately. The meeting resulted in an executive order that banned discrimination in all war industries. Signed on June 25, 1941, it was the first presidential order on a racial matter since the Emancipation Proclamation of 1863.

Public and Private Tragedies

Eleanor fought these battles at a time when she was suffering great personal pain. On September 7, 1941, Franklin's mother, Sara Delano Roosevelt, died at age 87. Franklin asked Eleanor not to change anything in the Roosevelt family home at Hyde Park, but to leave it just as Sara had left it. Days later, Eleanor rushed to the bedside of her beloved brother, Hall. For two weeks, she comforted him and watched as he slowly died of the same disease that had killed their father—alcoholism.

Photo courtesy of Library of Congress, LC-USW33-373-ZC.

General Benjamin O. Davis inspecting his troops in 1942.

Integrated:
A mix of races, genders, and ethnic groups, to whom services are equally available.

Emancipation Proclamation:
An order issued by President Abraham Lincoln in 1863 that freed all slaves held in southern slave-holding states.

Photo courtesy of Franklin Roosevelt Library, NPx 63-203.

Eleanor with her brother, Hall, in 1935.

The bombing of Pearl Harbor, December 7, 1941.

Photo courtesy of Library of Congress, LC-USW33-38582-ZC.

Minorities:
Members of racial, religious, political, or national groups that are smaller in number than the larger group of which they are a part.

Prejudices:
Negative behavior or exclusion directed at a person because of his or her race, religion, gender, disability, or nationality.

Eleanor had little time to grieve. On December 7, Japanese war planes bombed the American naval base at Pearl Harbor, Hawaii. In a matter of minutes, the bombing crippled 18 warships and destroyed 190 planes. Almost 2,400 people died in the attack. Another 1,178 were wounded.

That afternoon, while Franklin wrote his request for a Declaration of War, Eleanor addressed the nation by radio: "We know what we have to face[,] and we know that we are ready to face it." Americans had to prepare for a war on two fronts: one in the islands of the Pacific, and the other on the battlefields of Europe.

A two-front war required massive mobilization. Government-directed factories churned out airplanes, battleships, uniforms, weapons, and ammunition, ending unemployment and the Depression. From 1941 to 1944, employment in war industries tripled to 18 million laborers. More than 6 million of the new workers were women. Another 2 million were minorities—mostly due to the work of A. Philip Randolph.

Eleanor made it her job to see that women and minorities were treated fairly in war industry jobs. She toured factories and asked pointed questions. She beamed whenever male supervisors reported that women were "doing a swell job." Her faith in integration grew whenever a white worker praised a black worker. Still, as Eleanor discovered, old prejudices die hard. She never stopped her battle for equal rights for all citizens.

A Mockery of Justice

Eleanor was personally embarrassed by the treatment of Japanese Americans during the war. During the anti-Japanese backlash that followed the bombing of Pearl Harbor, Eleanor challenged the nation to continue to respect Japanese Americans. She told Franklin: "Being bitter against an American because of the actions of the country of his predecessors, does not make for unity and the winning of the war."

Responding to public pressure, Franklin signed Executive Order 9066, forcing all people of Japanese heritage to move from areas along the West Coast into internment camps. Franklin's decision stunned Eleanor. In a speech to the nation, she confessed that she could "not bear to think of children behind barbed wire looking out at the free world."

In 1942, protests broke out in some of the internment camps. Franklin asked Eleanor to visit the Gila River camp in Arizona. Eleanor's report on conditions in the camp helped to convince Franklin that internment threatened American civil liberties. Franklin would not admit that the camps had been a mistake, but he did agree to allow some Japanese-American men to enlist in a special European combat unit.

Eleanor thought the decision to send the Nisei troops to war while keeping their families imprisoned was an even greater mockery of justice. An official apology for Japanese internment did not come until 1988, 26 years after Eleanor's death. Togo Tanaka, the organizer of the protest at the Manzanar Internment Camp, named his first-born child after the first lady, in honor of her early recognition of the injustices suffered by Japanese Americans during the war.

Eleanor visiting a Japanese relocation camp in Gila River, Arizona, in 1943.

Internment camps:
Centers where the United States imprisoned U.S. citizens of Japanese heritage during World War II.

Nisei:
Persons born in the United States to parents of Japanese origin.

Winston Churchill.

Admiral William Halsey and other American military officials, standing in front of a plane named for Mrs. Roosevelt, welcome her to a World War II air base in 1943.

Goodwill Ambassador

Outraged by Eleanor's protests on behalf of minorities, some of her critics called her "unpatriotic" in a time of national crisis. Some even asked J. Edgar Hoover, the head of the FBI, to do something to keep Eleanor quiet. Franklin's advisers suggested that he give the first lady a war-related job to do. Taking their advice, Franklin sent Eleanor on a number of overseas trips.

In October 1942, Eleanor became the nation's goodwill ambassador to war-torn England. For weeks, she followed a schedule that exhausted most reporters. She stayed up late at night talking with British prime minister Winston Churchill. She toured bomb shelters and Red Cross centers. She visited U.S. Army camps. Whenever soldiers saw her, they shouted, "Hi, Eleanor!" Over cups of coffee, she promised the troops warmer socks and faster mail.

The following year, Franklin asked Eleanor to tour military bases in the Pacific. When Winston Churchill heard about the trip, he asked Eleanor: "Who is going with you?" She replied: "No one." In August 1943, the first lady boarded a plane by herself. She carried a single suitcase, saying that a Red Cross uniform was clothing enough.

Admiral William F. "Bull" Halsey, commander of the Pacific Fleet, dreaded the first lady's arrival. The hard-boiled career officer felt that Eleanor would be nothing but trouble. He quickly changed his mind. As Eleanor bravely ventured into war zones such as Guadalcanal, Halsey wrote: "I was ashamed of my original surliness." Eleanor, he added, had accomplished more good "than any other person . . . who had passed through my area."

By the time Eleanor returned home, she had visited 17 Pacific islands and covered a distance of more than 25,000 miles. Critics who had hoped the travels would quiet Eleanor's call for equality were mistaken. She felt stronger than ever that every American had equal rights to full citizenship.

Making Peace

As the 1944 election approached, Eleanor accepted the inevitable: "As long as the war was on it was a foregone conclusion that Franklin, if he was well enough, would run again."

The war had taken its toll on Franklin. His face was thin, his skin was pale, and his eyes were sunken, but he saw hope of victory. In a startling betrayal, Germany had attacked the Soviet Union in June 1941. The Allies, realizing that Soviet troops could help them, had welcomed the Communist nation into their alliance. With Soviet troops fighting the Germans on the eastern front, the Allies focused on winning the war in western Europe.

By November 1944, voters saw hope, too. They gave Franklin a fourth term in office. The election was a mandate for Franklin to win the war and negotiate terms of peace.

U.S. soldiers landing in Normandy, France, at the D-Day invasion, June 6, 1944.

Top: Eleanor in a South Pacific military hospital, at the bedside of a wounded African-American soldier in 1943.

Mandate:

An authoritative command or instruction.

Photo courtesy of Franklin Roosevelt Library, NPx 48-22:3659(68).

Franklin meets with Winston Churchill and Joseph Stalin at Yalta in 1945, to draw up the plans for world peace.

Photo courtesy of Franklin Roosevelt Library, NPx 46-11:1(4).

Franklin Roosevelt's funeral procession in Washington, D.C., April 14, 1945.

In February 1945, one month after his inauguration, Franklin made an exhausting trip to the city of Yalta in the Soviet Union to meet with Winston Churchill and Joseph Stalin, the Soviet premier. Together, they hammered out agreements for the postwar period. When Franklin reported on the meeting to the Senate, he spoke sitting down. His "thin and worn" appearance shocked many senators.

As the war drew to a close, Franklin shared his dream for the future with Eleanor. He said he would like to live in the Middle East or Asia—regions of the world where nations were struggling to be free. "I believe I could help," he said. Eleanor laughed: "Can't you think of something harder to do?" In fact, both Eleanor and Franklin had been working hard to lay the groundwork for an international peacekeeping organization—to fulfill the dreams of President Wilson's League of Nations. This dream would not be fully realized until the formation of the United Nations after the war.

A short time after Franklin shared his dream with Eleanor, she said good-bye to him as he headed off to Warm Springs for a rest. In a letter, she cheerfully wrote: "I hope you'll weigh 170 pounds when you return. Devotedly, E.R." These were the last words she wrote to him. On April 12, 1945, Eleanor lost her partner of more than 40 years. Franklin's death came unexpectedly, but peacefully.

"The story's over," said Eleanor to a reporter. But she was wrong. Only the partnership had ended. Her story as "First Lady of the World" was just beginning.

Epilogue

1945 - 1962

Key Events in Eleanor Roosevelt's Life 1945-1962

1945 President Truman appoints Eleanor to represent the United States at the newly formed United Nations.

1946 Eleanor visits Germany and talks with survivors of the Nazi Holocaust.

1947 Eleanor meets with Thurgood Marshall and other civil-rights leaders.

1948 Eleanor wins passage of the Universal Declaration of Human Rights. Meeting Golda Meir, Eleanor threatens to resign from the UN if the United States fails to recognize Israel.

1950 Eleanor resigns from the UN when Republican Dwight Eisenhower becomes president. She actively campaigns for Adlai Stevenson, the Democratic nominee for president, and opposes the House Un-American Activities Committee, led by Senator Joseph McCarthy.

1952

1953 Eleanor visits Hiroshima, Japan, and talks with Japanese leaders about the war.

1954 The chorus from the Wiltwick School for Boys serenades Eleanor on her 70th birthday. Eleanor praises
1955 the Supreme Court ruling in *Brown v. Board of Education*.

1956 Eleanor campaigns again for Democratic presidential candidate Adlai Stevenson. She meets with Rosa
1957 Parks, who triggered the Montgomery bus boycott.

Eleanor speaks out against apartheid in South Africa. She supports the passage of the Civil Rights Act and the integration of Central High School in Little Rock, Arkansas.

959
960 Russian premier Nikita Khrushchev visits Eleanor at Val-Kill.

961 Eleanor meets John F. Kennedy for the first time. He asks for her support for his presidential campaign.

962 President Kennedy appoints Eleanor to the UN Commission on Women and to a commission on civil-rights cases.

Eleanor invites Dr. Martin Luther King Jr. to discuss civil rights with her on nationwide TV. She collapses before the interview can be held and dies of tuberculosis in New York City at the age of 78. Four presidents attend her funeral.

1965

1970

EPILOGUE

"Life is meant to be lived," Eleanor Roosevelt once said. Franklin's death launched a new phase of her life, arguing the cause of freedom with Communist leaders and with those establishing new nations in Asia and the Middle East. At home, she advised presidents, championed the civil-rights movement, and followed her lifelong love: teaching young people.

Eleanor's proudest achievement came in 1948, when she helped draft the Universal Declaration of Human Rights—a global bill of rights—while serving as the first U.S. delegate to the United Nations. Eleanor's commitment to the declaration led to her support for the creation of Israel as a Jewish homeland.

After Eleanor entered her 70s, friends and family begged her to slow down. She replied: "When you cease to make a contribution you begin to die."

One morning in the spring of 1962, her secretary found her humming freedom songs from the civil-rights movement. Eleanor commented: "I had the most wonderful dream last night. . . . I was marching and singing and sitting in with students in the South." Eleanor never got the chance to fulfill that dream. On November 7, 1962, she died at age 78.

For the 18 years following Franklin's death, Eleanor lived more fully than most people do in a lifetime. She inspired generations of young women. As a teenage girl in Tennessee put it: "After all Mrs. Roosevelt has done, I'm not ashamed of being a girl anymore."

Eleanor addressing the United Nations General Assembly.

Eleanor meeting with civil-rights leaders (from left to right) James McClendon, Walter White, Roy Wilkins, and Thurgood Marshall in 1947.

Sources for Quotations

The following sources provided the quotations in this book. Specific page references are listed in the Teacher's Guide for *Eleanor Roosevelt: Freedom's Champion.*

Black, Allida M., *Casting Her Own Shadow*
Black, Ruby, *Eleanor Roosevelt*
Chadakoff, Rochelle, ed., *Eleanor Roosevelt's My Day*
Cook, Blanche Wiesen, *Eleanor Roosevelt: Volume I*
Hickok, Lorena, *Eleanor Roosevelt: Reluctant First Lady*
Kearney, James R., *Anna Eleanor Roosevelt*

Lash, Joseph P., *Eleanor and Franklin*
———, *"Life Was Meant to Be Lived"*
———, *Love, Eleanor*
Roosevelt, Eleanor, *This I Remember*
———, *This Is My Story*
Roosevelt, Elliott, and James Brough, *Mother R*
Ware, Susan, *Letter to the World*

Acknowledgments

The editors wish to thank the following individuals for their valuable assistance in the preparation of this book:
Seventh-grade social studies students at Burgundy Farm Country Day School, Alexandria, Virginia
Franklin Roosevelt Library, Mark Renovitch and staff
James Madison University Library
Smith College Library
Station KDKA in Pittsburgh, Pennsylvania
The Library of Congress, Washington, D.C.
The Maryland Historical Society
The National Archives, Washington, D.C.
Vassar College Library

Additional Photo Credits

cover image, Photo courtesy of Franklin Roosevelt Library, NPx 48-22:4280.
page 4, Photo courtesy of Franklin Roosevelt Library, NPx 64-165.
page 7, Photo courtesy of Franklin Roosevelt Library, NPx 63 485.
page 16, Photo courtesy of Library of Congress, LC-USZ64-4637.
page 24, Photo courtesy of Library of Congress, LC-USZ62-57005.
page 35, Photo courtesy of Franklin Roosevelt Library, NPx 47-96:882.
page 36, Photo courtesy of National Archives, 306-NT-9156.
page 46, Photo courtesy of Library of Congress, LC-USZ62-75334.
page 58, Photo courtesy of Library of Congress, LC-USZ62-7095.
page 69, Photo courtesy of Franklin Roosevelt Library, NPx 47-96:767.

page 70, Photo courtesy of Library of Congress, LC-USZ62-13672.
page 80, Photo courtesy of Library of Congress, LC-USF33-30193 M1.
page 91, Photo courtesy of National Archives, 306-NT-341F-88.
page 107, *Norfolk & Western Magazine* photo courtesy of Franklin Roosevelt Library, NPx 56-563(15).
page 117, Photo courtesy of Franklin Roosevelt Library.
page 117, Omicron (DR) photo courtesy of Franklin Roosevelt Library, NPx 55-592(17).
page 118, Photo courtesy of Franklin Roosevelt Library, NPx 65-733.
end papers, Robert Dumke photo, © the *Milwaukee Journal,* 1936, reproduced with permission.

Bibliography

Black, Allida M. *Casting Her Own Shadow: Eleanor Roosevelt and the Shaping of Postwar Liberalism*. New York: Columbia University Press, 1996.

Black, Ruby. *Eleanor Roosevelt: A Biography*. New York: Duell, Sloan, and Pearce, 1940.

Caroli, Betty Boyd. *First Ladies*. New York: Oxford University Press, 1995.

Chadakoff, Rochelle, ed. *Eleanor Roosevelt's My Day: Her Acclaimed Columns, 1936-1945*. New York: Pharos Books, 1989.

Cook, Blanche Wiesen. *Eleanor Roosevelt: Volume I, 1884-1933*. New York: Penguin Books, 1992.

Emblidge, David, ed. *Eleanor Roosevelt's My Day: Her Acclaimed Columns, 1946-1952*. New York: Pharos Books, 1990.

Freedman, Russell. *Eleanor Roosevelt: A Life of Discovery*. New York: Clarion Books, 1993.

Freidel, Frank, ed. *Eleanor Roosevelt's My Day: Volume III, First Lady of the World, 1953-1962*. New York: Pharos Books, 1991.

Goodwin, Doris Kearns. *No Ordinary Time*. New York: Simon & Schuster, 1994.

Gurewitsch, A. David. *Eleanor Roosevelt: Her Day, A Personal Album*. New York: Quadrangle Books, 1974.

Hershan, Stella K. *The Candles She Lit: The Legacy of Eleanor Roosevelt*. Westport, Conn.: Praeger, 1993.

Hickok, Lorena A. *Eleanor Roosevelt: Reluctant First Lady*. New York: Dodd, Mead, 1980.

Hoff-Wilson, Joan, and Marjorie Lightman, eds. *Without Precedent: The Life and Career of Eleanor Roosevelt*. Bloomington: Indiana University Press, 1984.

Horton, Aimee Isgrig. *The Highlander Folk School: A History of Its Major Programs, 1932-1961*. Brooklyn, N.Y.: Carlson, 1989.

Horton, Myles, and Paulo Freire. *We Make the Road by Walking: Conversations on Education and Social Change*. Philadelphia: Temple University Press, 1990.

Kearney, James R. *Anna Eleanor Roosevelt: The Evolution of a Reformer*. Boston: Houghton Mifflin, 1968.

Lash, Joseph P. *Eleanor and Franklin*. New York: W. W. Norton, 1971.

———. *"Life Was Meant to Be Lived."* New York: W. W. Norton, 1984.

———. *Love, Eleanor*. Garden City, N.Y.: Doubleday, 1982.

———. *A World of Love*. Garden City, N.Y.: Doubleday, 1984.

———. *The Years Alone*. New York: W. W. Norton, 1972.

MacLeish, Archibald. *The Eleanor Roosevelt Story*. Boston: Houghton Mifflin, 1965.

Roosevelt, Eleanor. *The Autobiography of Eleanor Roosevelt*. New York: Da Capo Press, 1992.

———. *On My Own*. New York: Harper & Brothers, 1958.

———. *This I Remember*. New York: Harper & Brothers, 1949.

———. *This Is My Story*. New York: Harper & Brothers, 1937.

———. *Tomorrow Is Now*. New York: Harper & Row, 1963.

———. *You Learn by Living*. New York: Harper & Brothers, 1960.

Roosevelt, Elliott, and James Brough. *Mother R: Eleanor Roosevelt's Untold Story*. New York: Putnam, 1977.

Scharf, Lois. *Eleanor Roosevelt: First Lady of American Liberalism*. Boston: Twayne Publishers, 1987.

Skarmeas, Nancy J., ed. *Great Americans: Eleanor Roosevelt*. Nashville: Ideals Publications, 1997.

Ware, Susan. *Letter to the World: Seven Women Who Shaped the American Century*. New York: W. W. Norton, 1998.

Index

TIME LIFE EDUCATION Time Life Education Inc. is a division of Time Life Inc.

TIME LIFE INC.
PRESIDENT AND CEO: George Artandi

TIME LIFE EDUCATION INC.
PRESIDENT: Mary Davis Holt

Time-Life History Makers
ELEANOR ROOSEVELT: FREEDOM'S CHAMPION

Managing Editor: Mary J. Wright
Editorial Director: Bonnie H. Hobson

Authors: Deborah A. Parks and Melva L. Ware
Deborah A. Parks graduated from the State University of New York at Stony Brook and completed graduate studies at the City College of New York and Columbia University. She has taught social studies and history at the middle school, high school, and college levels and is a seasoned writer and editor. While growing up in Hyde Park, Deborah was able to meet Eleanor Roosevelt and to share stories with people who knew her.

Melva L. Ware is a graduate of Spelman College in Atlanta, Georgia. She is an assistant professor in the Division of Teaching and Learning, School of Education, University of Missouri-St. Louis. Dr. Ware is a former middle school language arts and social studies teacher and high school English and humanities teacher.

Text Editors: Allan Fallow, Phil Berardelli
Picture Research: Joan Marie Mathys, Ben F. Collins
Associate Editor/Research and Writing: Laura Heinle
Picture Associate: Angela Bailey
Editorial Assistant: Maria Washington
Editorial Interns: Renesa Bell, Marin Graney, Marquita McLin, Rosaura Plummer, Lenese Stephens, Tonya Wilson
Student Researcher: Heather Jurgensen
Technical Art Specialist: John Drummond
Designed by: Susan Angrisani and Howard Smith, Designsmith, Inc.
Senior Copyeditor: Judith Klein
Indexer: Sunday Oliver, Green River Indexing
Correspondents: Christina Lieberman (New York), Maria Vincenza Aloisi, (Paris)

Pre-press service by the Time-Life Imaging Center

Vice President of Marketing and Publisher: Rosalyn McPherson Perkins
Directors of Book Production: Marjann Caldwell, Patricia Pascale
Director of Publishing Technology: Betsi McGrath
Director of Photography and Research: John Conrad Weiser
Production Managers: Carolyn Clark, Carolyn Bounds
Quality Assurance Manager: James King
Chief Librarian: Louise D. Forstall

Consultant: Ben F. Collins

Teacher Review Board: Barbara Adeboye, seventh-grade social studies teacher, Thomas Jefferson Middle School, Arlington, Va.; Tia Hawkins, fifth-grade teacher, Overlook Elementary School, Prince Georges County, Md.; Rozena Killen-Johnson, reading specialist, George Washington Middle School, Alexandria, Va.; Mary Lou Guthrie, seventh-grade social studies teacher, Burgundy Farm Country Day School, Alexandria, Va.

©1999 Time Life Inc. All rights reserved. No part of this book may be reproduced in any form or by any electronic or mechanical means, including information storage and retrieval devices or systems, without prior written permission from the publisher, except that brief passages may be quoted for reviews.

First printing. Printed in U.S.A.
School and library distribution by Time-Life Education, P.O. Box 85026, Richmond, Virginia 23285-5026.
Telephone: 1-800-449-2010   Internet: www.timelifeedu.com

TIME-LIFE is a trademark of Time Warner Inc. U.S.A.

Library of Congress Cataloging-in-Publication Data

Parks, Deborah A., 1948–
    Eleanor Roosevelt: freedom's champion / Deborah A. Parks and Melva L. Ware.
        p. cm.—(Time-Life history makers)
    Includes bibliographical references and index.
    Summary: Examines the life and accomplishments of the First Lady who devoted herself to helping others and working for peace.
    ISBN 0-7835-5441-9
    1. Roosevelt, Eleanor, 1884-1962—Juvenile literature. 2. Presidents' spouses—United States Biography—Juvenile literature. 3. United States—Politics and government —1933-1945—Juvenile literature.
[1. Roosevelt, Eleanor, 1884-1962. 2. First ladies. 3. Women Biography.]
I. Ware, Melva Lawson, 1951–   . II. Title. III. Series.
E807.1.R48P37   1999
973.917'092—dc21   99-24897
[B]   CIP

Whereas recognition of the inherent dignity and of the equal and inalienable rights of all members of the hu

Whereas recognition of the inherent dignity and of the equal and inalienable rights of all members of the h

rights have resulted in barbarous acts which have outraged the conscience of mankind, and the advent of a wo

rights have resulted in barbarous acts which have outraged the conscience of mankind, and the advent of a

proclaimed as the highest aspiration of the common people, Whereas it is essential, if man is not to be comp

proclaimed as the highest aspiration of the common people, Whereas it is essential, if man is not to be com

protected by the rule of law, Whereas it is essential to promote the development of friendly relations betwee

protected by the rule of law, Whereas it is essential to promote the development of friendly relations betwe

human rights, in the dignity and worth of the human person and in the equal rights of men and women and h

human rights, in the dignity and worth of the human person and in the equal rights of men and women and h

have pledged themselves to achieve, in cooperation with the United Nations, the promotion of universal resp

have pledged themselves to achieve, in cooperation with the United Nations, the promotion of universal res

and freedoms is of the greatest importance for the full realization of this pledge, Now, therefore, The Gene

importance for the full rea re, The Gener

all peoples and all nations, to the end that every individual and every organ of society, keeping this Declar

ation and that every individual and his Declaratic

and by progressive measures, national and international, to secure their universal and effective recognition an

and by progressive measure ternational, to secure their universal and effective recognition

their jurisdiction.

their jurisdiction.